An Introduction to Credit Scoring

by

Edward M. Lewis

© 1992 Edward M. Lewis
Published by
Fair, Isaac and Co., Inc.
120 N. Redwood Drive
San Rafael, California 94903-1996 USA
1-800-999-2955
1-415-472-2211

Printed and Bound in the
United States

Library of Congress Catalog Number: 90-92258

Second Edition

Table of Contents

II.2.9 Continued

III.3 Continued

List of Figures

Preface

This book is being written to fill what I feel is a conspicuous gap in the information available about the world of credit. Credit scoring has been in use for thirty years but almost nothing has been written about it either for the general public or for the people who work in the field. While various papers have been written about individual aspects of scoring, there is no single or convenient source for general information about the ideas behind it, or what is involved in developing and using a scoring system.

Both the public and the credit industry have been penalized by this lack of information. Horror stories appear from time to time in the press about imagined evils of credit scoring, while many credit professionals hesitate to investigate the opportunities of scoring or fail to use it profitably because there is no convenient source for the information they need. Also, there are many people entering the workplace who know nothing about credit scoring but who have no source of information.

There are various reasons for this lack of a basic coverage of scoring. One is that the subject matter changes rapidly. Another is that most of the manufacturers of credit scoring tools have been busy and have had no time to do anything not directly connected with their company's business. In the past they have had neither the inclination nor the motivation to provide what might be considered secrets to their competitors. While each manufacturer has its own proprietary procedures, there are basic ideas that are common to all scoring system producers, and those are the ideas that are discussed in this book.

I had the privilege of being in on the development of scoring almost from the very beginning. I joined Fair, Isaac and Company, Incorporated in 1960, just as that company, then only a handful of people, was making one of its first scoring systems. Since that time I have watched the credit scoring industry come into existence. It has been an exciting time. The invention of a new financial tool and its introduction into the commercial world may sound boring, but it is hardly that to those who are trying to do it. Since 1960 I have had the opportunity to take part in the production of a large number of scoring systems, and I have also had a hand in the development of the processes involved in scoring system production. I have been closely associated with the problems of marketing scoring and of educating the credit industry in the new ideas. During those years I was one of the people too busy to write any extensive document for general use, although I felt the need for it all along.

I am now retired, so I can write what I please. I no longer have the pressure of the need to produce revenue, nor do I feel the obligation of a "company man" to get agreement from all my colleagues before I publish anything. As a result, this book is my own. I use terminology that appeals to me, and the views and opinions I present are my own. The faults and errors in the book are entirely mine; I have not submitted it for anyone's approval.

While the faults and errors are all mine, the debts I owe to my colleagues are enormous. William R. Fair and Earl J. Isaac founded their company in 1956 and began to investigate the possibility of applying statistical methods to the field of consumer credit shortly thereafter. It has been my good fortune to learn the business from them and from others who joined the company as time went on. Robert D. Sanderson, John D. Woldrich, Gerald de Kerchove, Larry E. Rosenberger, O. D. Nelson and Mary Hopper are among the many who have had roles in the continuing development of the field of scoring, and all of them have taught me valuable lessons.

I owe special thanks to Emmanuel Uren. His generous contribution of technical knowledge and of editorial talent has improved both the technical content and the overall presentation of the material in this book. The inadequacies that remain must be charged entirely to my account.

This book is not a treatise on the technical construction of credit scoring tables or on the statistical methods that are employed by the various producers of these tables. It is a discussion of how certain specific analytical methods can be applied to the management of a credit portfolio, a discussion that can be followed by a newcomer to the business but that can also be of use to experienced credit people with on-going responsibilities, as well as to senior managers who may not have day-to-day contact with the subject.

As I have said, this book cannot claim to be up-to-date. Even while it is being written new ideas are being developed, and after it is complete that process will continue. However, I feel that the ideas that underlie scoring are of general validity, no matter what new developments may appear, and that these ideas should be understood by anyone involved in credit either as a user or a supplier.

Since I have been an employee of only one of the manufacturers of credit scoring tools, most of my comments are colored by that experience. I do not know the details of what any of the companies other than my former employers do in the course of their work, but I am confident that the overall nature of what they do is sufficiently similar to my own experience that the statements I make have general validity. There are, I have no doubt, differences in detail, but I think that the thrust of all manufacturers is the same. The problems faced in the installation and use of scoring systems are common to most situations and are largely independent of the manufacturer of the scoring system that is involved.

In Part I of this book I have included a certain amount of information about the history of credit and the background against which credit scoring developed that is not immediately germane to the problem of understanding credit scoring. As a result, Part I can be skipped by anyone who doesn't much care about either subject and wants to get right into the meat of the matter.

I hope the readers will find this book of value, and I will appreciate any comments or corrections that anyone has to suggest.

Preface to Second Edition

I am fortunate in having the opportunity to publish a second edition. This lets me correct the typographical errors that appeared in the first edition, hoping that I am not introducing new ones in the process.

More important, it also gives me the opportunity to benefit from the advice and suggestions of individuals who were kind enough to read the first edition critically and to note the items that merited either correction or amplification. I am particularly indebted to Martin Sleath, whose careful reading has allowed me to correct some errors and to better explain some statements. As usual, I have used my own judgment in these matters, so that any remaining inaccuracies or inadequacies are entirely due to me.

For technical reasons involving how second editions are produced, I have placed an Addendum to this edition at the end. Wherever the symbol ★ appears in the text, please refer to the Addendum for additional comment.

Introduction

What is now generally understood to be "credit scoring" is a process whereby some information about a credit applicant or a credit account is converted into numbers that are then combined (usually added) to form a score. This score is a measure of the creditworthiness of the individual concerned.[1] Figure 1 shows an example of what a credit scoring table might look like.

Figure 1

Example of Application Scoring Table					
Years on Job	Less than 6 Months **5**	Six Mos to 1 Yr 6 Mos **14**	1 Yr 7 Mo to 6 Yr 8 Mo. **20**	6 Yrs 9 Mo to 10 Yr 5 Mo. **27**	10 Yrs 6 Mos or More **39**	
Own or Rent	Own or Buying **40**	Rent **19**	All Other **26**			
Banking	Checking Account **22**	Savings Account **17**	Checking and Savings **31**	None **0**		
Major Credit Card	Yes **27**	No **11**				
Occupation	Retired **41**	Professional **36**	Clerical **27**	Sales **18**	Service **12**	All Other **27**
Age of Applicant	18 to 25 **19**	26 to 31 **14**	32 to 34 **22**	35 to 51 **26**	52 to 61 **34**	62 and Over **40**
Worst Credit Reference	Major Derogatory **-15**	Minor Derogatory **-4**	No Record **-2**	One Satisfactory **9**	Two or More Satisfactory **18**	No Investig. **0**

[1] I am using the word "Creditworthiness" here because everyone thinks he or she understands it. I will discuss this more fully later, since in reality people understand that word in very different ways. For the present, let us take it to mean the credit risk presented by an applicant.

The purpose of this book is to discuss why credit scoring came about, how credit scoring tables are developed (with a minimum of mathematics), and how they can be used. It is intended to be a book for a range of readers; for someone who is just curious about the subject, for someone who is entering the credit industry and would like some general education, and for people experienced in the credit industry who would like additional information about one of the most important tools that they can apply in their work.

The history of credit scoring is, like most good ideas, lost in a confusion of legend and folklore. Almost certainly many organizations and individuals made attempts to quantify the process of credit decision at times in the past, but very little of a practical nature was done until after the Second World War.

When that war ended, a number of events took place that permitted the development of credit scoring as it is now generally understood. Computers became available for commercial purposes, the new field of Operations Research encouraged quantitative examination of all sorts of business situations, and more and more people became adept in modern statistical methods. In addition, the end of the war brought enormous changes in the economies of almost all of the countries of the world, bringing all sorts of new problems to business managements. The field of credit was no exception.

Credit is probably as old as commerce. The need for funds for investment or to cover a temporary cash shortage must have occurred early in the development of civilization. Ancient Babylon, as early as 2000 B.C. already had a well developed banking system that extended credit. A stone tablet of that time states: "Two shekels of silver have been borrowed by Mas-Schamach, the son of Adadrimeni, from the Sun priestess Amat-Schamach, the daughter of Warad-Enlil. He will pay the Sun-God's interest. At the time of the harvest he will pay back the sum and the interest upon it."

Both ancient Greece and Rome had well developed banking and credit institutions, despite the fact that the computation of interest with Greek or Roman number systems must have been a burden.

The subsequent development of the nations of Europe and, later, the Americas, brought with it increasingly complex commerce and a corresponding increase in the need for and the use of commercial credit. As a rule, this credit was secured by goods, often left in the custody of the creditor, or by real property.

Personal unsecured credit was in limited supply and was most readily available to princes and potentates, who offered the credit grantors the choice between unsecured credit and confiscation. Personal credit for ordinary people was available in very limited forms, the most common of which was the pawn shop. These offered secured rather than unsecured credit. Goods were deposited in the pawn shop for specified intervals and at varying rates.

The very earliest pawn shops, established somewhat before the year 1200 A.D., were charitable institutions and charged no interest. This quickly changed, and although some interest-free pawnshops continued to exist for many years, by 1350 commercial pawn shops, charging interest, were being established around Europe. Most European countries and many of the nations of Latin America still have state operated pawn shops that will lend on almost anything and charge only modest interest.

The development of interest-charging pawn shops brought on a long controversy as to the morality of charging interest, a controversy that continues to this day. This dispute was solved, at least for some, by the invention of the dubious distinction between interest and usury.

The gradual rise of the middle class brought with it a demand for what we now call consumer credit. The more affluent members of the middle class in England developed, in cooperation with their bankers, the concept of a banking overdraft, which was nothing more than a loan by another name. In the United States the overdraft idea did not catch on, but the need for personal credit called for a response, which came in the form of the Small Loan Company or Finance Company, credit providers that remain a major component of the industry.

The Finance Company received a strong stimulus with the development of the Model T Ford. This vehicle could be purchased by a very wide segment of the population but was, nonetheless, a major investment. At first the banks looked at lending money secured by an automobile as a poor business, since unlike a house, a car could be driven away never to return, a problem we still have. The Finance Companies filled the gap left by the banks in this area and experienced a rapid growth.

While the Finance Companies were blossoming in the early years of the 20th century, they still were not providing as much credit, especially unsecured credit, as the demand called for. This was partly from natural caution regarding unsecured lending and partly because of the occurrence of the First World War and, fifteen years later, the Great Depression.

The end of the Second World War brought about enormous changes in society all over the world. In the United States commerce and industry grew with great speed. People throughout the country began to move about at a rate never before seen. People began to feel the need for personal credit and the demand for it began to grow.

The demand for expanded consumer credit came at a time when all the conditions that would allow the desired expansion became available. Capital free for investment in credit portfolios was available. Credit scoring, making it possible to process very large numbers of requests for credit, was developed. Automated credit bureaus, making available enormous files of credit information, were being formed. The communications necessary to support all of the demands were being installed. What we now know as consumer credit came into being.

PART I

The Background and History of Scoring

I.1 - Background.

I.1.1 - The Nature of Consumer Credit.

Introduction. The experienced credit professional should review, from time to time, some of the background of consumer credit and, perhaps, re-consider some long-held opinions. For the newcomer in the credit industry, regardless of the level of the position, it is helpful to learn something about the business and how it has been developed in the past twenty or thirty years.

This part of this book reviews some subjects of importance to the credit industry. Starting with a definition of consumer credit, the discussion goes on to the concept of risk, and reviews some of the mythology that has grown up in the credit industry. This is followed by a brief look of those aspects of credit that are concerned with the determination and control of risk and a discussion of the motivation of the credit industry to change from the traditional methods of risk evaluation and control to methods based on empirical evidence and modern statistical techniques.

Consumer Credit. The term "Consumer Credit" is broadly understood to mean any of the many forms of commerce under which an individual obtains money or goods or services on condition of a promise to repay the money or to pay for the goods or services, along with a fee (the interest) at some specific future date or dates.

There is more to consumer credit than a simple definition. Currently, consumer credit is an industry in its own right, not merely the incidental adjunct of other enterprises. While some organizations, most of them retailers, consider their credit operations to be subordinate to sales, many, if not most, credit grantors look on their credit departments as profit centers. Consumer credit has become an enormous industry. In the United States in 1989, the total amount of outstanding consumer credit was over 700 billion dollars.[1] At the present stage of development of Western society, credit is no longer looked on as a luxury or a privilege, it is widely regarded as a right and as a

---

[1] According to the Federal Reserve Bank of San Francisco. This figure does not include home mortgages.

facility that is essential to the good life.

The Soviet Union and the countries of eastern Europe as well as China are beginning to see the utility of consumer credit as a stimulus to production and economic expansion, and these countries can be expected to make great progress in the field over the next few decades as they develop their facilities for the production of consumer goods.

Today consumer credit is an essential enterprise. A major task of this industry is to make credit widely available, so that as many people as possible can have the opportunity to make use of this powerful tool. This is not only a socially desirable goal, but an equally valuable economic one; the consumer credit industry is profitable, and the broader its base becomes and the more extensive the use of credit becomes, the more profitable the industry will be.

While credit is now widely available, there are still many people who cannot get it. This is a problem for the credit industry as well as for the people concerned. One of the important privileges of the middle class is the availability of credit, and as long as someone finds credit unobtainable, that person is denied many of the benefits of our abundant society. The credit industry must find ways to make consumer credit available to everyone who will use it wisely, regardless of his or her place in the economic structure of the nation, in its own interest as well as that of society.

Risk. Inherent in the idea of credit, since it involves a promise to repay monies at some date in the future, is the idea of risk. The future is not predictable with perfect accuracy, so we must accept the fact to which both logic and experience testify, that not all debts will be paid as agreed. The best we can do is to make an imperfect prediction and estimate the degree of risk that is involved in each particular request for credit, and then to accept only those risks which we consider low enough so that, over a great many cases of grants of credit, our enterprise will prosper.

Until credit scoring made it possible to assign a numerical measure of risk to each application for credit, management had no way of expressing a corporate policy such as: "Accept only those applications whose risk is 13 to 1 or better".[1] As a result, each individual credit evaluator decided for himself what level of risk the applicant pre-

---

[1] The "odds quote" as used here means that out of 14 applicants for credit all having the same estimated risk, 13 will perform well and 1 will not.

sented and what level of risk the enterprise *as a whole* should tolerate. In a nation-wide loan company with, perhaps, 1000 offices, there might be as many as two to three thousand people defining overall corporate policy.

In using traditional methods the credit analysts did not take note of the fact (and may have been unaware) that they were answering two questions. The first question was: what is the risk presented by the applicant, and the second was: what is the maximum risk that the enterprise should accept. While it makes sense for the individual analyst to estimate the risk presented by any particular applicant, it makes no sense at all for each of a multiplicity of individual analysts to set his own version of the corporate goal. However, until a numerical risk-measuring process became available, there was no alternative.

This system, however illogical, worked fairly well for a long time. One of the reasons for its success, however, was that the credit industry was very conservative in its view of the highest acceptable risk, and as a result it acted (unintentionally) to impede the growth of consumer credit.

After World War II, when pressure developed for greatly expanded consumer credit, it became important to measure risk more effectively than had been possible in the past. Credit scoring arrived on the scene at just the right time.

"Creditworthiness". Creditworthiness is a word that appears frequently whenever the subject of credit comes up. People rarely take the time to ask just what it means. It is a word that has caused a great deal of trouble because no two people use exactly the same definition, although everyone is sure that he himself, or she herself, has it in abundance.

In theory, creditworthiness is a characteristic of an individual that makes him or her a suitable candidate for the extension of credit while someone who is not creditworthy is, conversely, unsuited to credit[1] This sounds fine at first hearing, but a moment's examination shows that it is a useless definition and that the use of the term "credit-

---

[1] In the interest of brevity, I will stop using "him or her" and "himself or herself" and stick to a single pronoun. In the past, the masculine noun has been used to cover both genders, and I see no reason to depart from that custom here, although the implied bias of the old custom has no part in today's world or in my own personal attitudes.

worthy" causes more trouble than it cures.

Creditworthiness is not a characteristic that is part of the genetic makeup of an individual. People are not born creditworthy or non-creditworthy. The vagaries of fate are too capricious to allow an individual to pay his debts (or not to) despite all of the other possible conditions of the world.[1] Anyone who has seen a handful of credit bureau reports knows that there are many individuals who have paid some of their obligations in an entirely satisfactory manner while failing to do so with others. These people are no doubt considered creditworthy by those they pay and non-creditworthy by those they don't.

The reasonable way to avoid the hazards of the word "creditworthy" is not to use it at all and to concentrate instead on risk. To tell someone he is not creditworthy is a personal attack that may very easily be resented, but to state that an individual represents a risk that your organization is unwilling to assume is not only far less offensive, it is, in fact, exactly the case.

Mythology. Every profession develops its own mythology over the years, and the credit industry is no exception. The idea of credit-worthiness is only one of the many aspects of that mythology. Most of the mythology of credit has grown up out of the experience of the many diverse people who have been involved in the industry.

A persistent myth in the credit industry is that loans are only made on the basis of the Three C's of Credit: Character, Capacity, and Collateral. Like many myths, this one has some foundation in fact. In older and simpler times, times when the population of the world remained fairly stable and people did not move around with any frequency, applicants for credit were well known to the individuals to whom they made application. These credit grantors, knowing the applicant, and having known him perhaps for years, had a fairly good idea of the individual's personality and general character. Furthermore, the credit grantor had a good estimate of the reliability of the income and

---

[1] It should be noted that it is a good thing that creditworthiness is not a genetically transmitted characteristic. Consider for a moment what society would be like if being creditworthy or not creditworthy were an inborn trait. Imagine being told that your adored four year old is, oh horror, not credit-worthy, even though you and your spouse and your other children are!! What would you do? You can't abandon the child, there is no operation that can be performed to graft creditworthiness on it. This child's future would be non-existent. Consider another case: one of your children, creditworthy from birth, brings home a non-creditworthy person and announces the intention to get married. What do you do?

of the ability of the applicant to pay his debts, and he could assess the value of any collateral offered.

Nowadays, none of this is the case. The decision maker of most credit grantors never sees the applicants and knows only what is available on the application and on any credit bureau report that is obtained. The decision maker has no way of evaluating the accuracy of any of the "facts" stated on the application.[1] There is, therefore, no way to estimate Character, unless that term is redefined to mean that the applicant has a reasonable record regarding other known debts, which is, at best, a poor definition of the word.

Capacity is now no easier to measure. The fact that an individual has a good income is no guarantee of capacity; the stated income may be false (or exaggerated) or he may have unreported debts. Any experienced collector can cite case after case of individuals with what looks like ample Capacity who pay very badly and other cases of individuals with the most modest Capacity who are on the dot every time. So much for Capacity. Today the lion's share of consumer credit is granted without Collateral, so this item, too, has lost any value it ever had. There is, then, nothing left of the "Three C's".

Another popular myth is that credit is extended only to those with the willingness and ability to pay. A bit of thought disposes of this myth, as well. Consider "ability to pay". Exactly what is this supposed to mean? Like Capacity in the Three C's, it appears to mean that there is sufficient income to pay the obligation. In the negative this may be true, if not very useful; if an individual has no income, no assets, and no intention of getting either, then extending credit to that individual can hardly be considered wise. In fact, no one would consider it at all, and no applicant in such a condition is likely to appear. Any real applicant will have, or at least claim, some income or some assets. Does this automatically mean that "ability to pay" exists? Well, maybe it does and maybe it doesn't. Even if the applicant has other debts, and even if those debts exceed his current income, it does not mean that he will not pay a new obligation. Of course, it doesn't mean that he will, either. Ability to pay is a weak reed to lean on.

---

[1] Some credit grantors still check the accuracy of statements on applications, but this is rare nowadays. In earlier times, credit grantors did a lot of checking, much of it by mail, a process that took a great deal of time. In those days people didn't seem to care if a decision on an application took a month or more. Today a wait of even a week produces an angry applicant.

"Willingness to pay" is even weaker. Has anyone ever had an applicant who asked for credit and stated that he was *un*willing to pay it back? I doubt it. Willingness is usually measured by looking at a credit report and seeing if previous obligations were met. The extreme cases are easy enough; if all debts were paid, it is not unreasonable to expect a new one to be paid. If all previous debts have been defaulted, it is again not unreasonable to hesitate to extend further funds. It is the wide middle ground that is shaky; how many good payments offset a bad case? Each analyst will have his own views on this matter, making usable general statements impossible. Worse, how can "willingness" be measured in cases where there is no history? Gazing deep into the applicant's eyes and weighing his soul was a task beyond human capability even in those earlier days when the applicant appeared in person. Now that the applicant appears only as a piece of disembodied paper, guesses about "willingness" are pointless.

A more complex and subtle myth, and one that has confused much of the discussion on the merits of scoring, is the myth of causality. There are people who are convinced that there is an underlying causal model to credit and that it is, therefore, possible to "know" what "causes" good credit behavior. People who hold this view reject the idea of scoring since, "knowing" as they do who will pay and who will not, scoring is not needed. When asked why someone they "knew" would pay in fact did not do so, the response is that, at the time of the decision it was "known" that the person would pay but that something happened later that caused the change. Even if this were true it would not be very helpful, since a credit grantor is not interested in unstable conditions; he is interested only in the fact of the timely repayment of the debt.

Causality is a dangerous myth. We have no absolute causal models for any aspect of human behavior. We do not "know" why one particular man becomes a criminal and another a cardinal. We do not "know" which individuals will succeed in some endeavor and which will fail. We do not "know" who will receive a Nobel Prize, who will become President. In fact we cannot "know" what any specific person will do in the future, yet there are those who claim that there is a causal model for credit performance! This leads to all sorts of strange conclusions, one being that items considered in a scoring system must

---

[1] On one occasion Fair, Isaac and Co. was actually accused of knowing how to make a "perfect" scoring system that would, without error, identify satisfactory applicants, but that we were concealing it so that we could sell a large number of "imperfect" scoring systems.

have what their proponents call "face validity". I have tried to find out just what "face validity" means and have concluded that it means a quality that satisfies the prejudices of the speaker.

A little thought about the nature of causality leads to the inescapable conclusion that we do not have any effective causal models for credit behavior. While it is possible that such a model may be found, none has been found so far, and I for one deny that such a model exists or can exist. Once we abandon the myth of a causal model, the only thing that remains is the associative model. An associative model is one that associates one or more phenomena with the phenomenon one hopes to predict. Since the model is associative, there is no claim of a causal link between the associated phenomena. In terms of credit, we are seeking to predict satisfactory credit behavior and we must seek whatever facts we can, however "unlikely", that are associated with subsequent payment performance.

Over the years creditors have established a body of information that they consider helpful in estimating the risk presented at the time of a credit decision. Not all credit grantors ask the same questions or ask for information in the same form, but in one way or another they all seek information regarding the applicant's living arrangements, his job, his income, his assets and liabilities, and his dependents. It is these facts, and any others that are made available, that credit scoring seeks to associate in a numerical way with later credit performance.[1]

I.1.2 Credit Risk Evaluation.

Once we dispose of the mythology of credit and the amusing, if sophomoric, shibboleths of the past, such as "Don't lend to Painters, Plumbers, or Paperhangers" and the many variants that I have heard over the years, we can look squarely at the very real problems faced by credit grantors and try to reach some useful conclusions.

The problem central to the granting of credit is the estimation of risk. If risk is estimated poorly, the entire enterprise can fail either because of excessive default or lack of business. If you can estimate risk better than your competitor can, his business is in danger, since you are able to offer better terms to more people than he is. Credit scoring is the tool designed to give credit management the ability to measure

---

[1] It would be interesting to examine other phenomena to see if any of them are associated strongly with satisfactory credit behavior, but it is not easy to persuade creditors to ask questions outside of the usual framework.

risk and to take the action best suited to each risk that is identified.

Before the invention of revolving credit, most credit was extended for relatively brief periods. Consequently, the decision to grant or not to grant credit, a decision made at the time an application was submitted, was regarded by many as the only credit decision. In fact, a number of credit decisions are made during the lifetime of an account, even one involving a short term loan. These decisions have become more apparent since the development of revolving credit as well as traditional credit on long terms.

The first decision, the one made at application time, remains of great importance. Credit scoring was originally developed to evaluate the risk presented by applicants, and this is still a major use of credit scoring systems.[1]

Other credit decisions that can be aided by scoring techniques have been present all along. One is the decision as to how to collect a delinquent account. The art of collections has been developed in many ways by many people throughout history. Most organizations of any size have collections departments and these have policies on how collections are to be handled. It is not uncommon to treat early delinquency with a statement overprint or a relatively mildly phrased letter. More serious delinquencies are handled either by less mildly phrased correspondence or by human collectors on the telephone. (Old timers in the business have marvelous stories to tell about collections when they were done in person. Much of what these collectors did in the "good old days" is now illegal, and regulations at various governmental levels now circumscribe what can and what cannot be done.)

Telephone collections can be highly effective, but the traditional procedure usually leaves each collector with a series of decisions

[1] When the ideas of credit scoring were being developed thirty years ago, we all used the term "credit scoring system" to refer to the completed product, which included the credit scoring table and the voluminous statistical information necessary for its effective use. A more exact term would be to describe the scoring table and the instructions for its use as a "scoring algorithm", and this is what Fair, Isaac and Co., Inc. now uses, since it feels that the precision of the term is more appropriate. I propose to use the term "credit scoring system" in this book because that is the way I think about it and the way many of my friends use the term. For purists, the formal definition of an algorithm, according to the dictionary, is: A procedure for solving a mathematical problem in a finite number of steps that frequently involves repetition of an operation; broadly: a step-by-step procedure for solving a problem or accomplishing some end.

regarding the best procedure to follow, decisions for which the collectors frequently have insufficient information. They have no way to measure the risk presented by a defaulting creditor, since there is no risk evaluation tool in the traditional case. Often collectors treat all of their collection accounts in the same way.

A second collections problem concerns accounts that are over their credit limit though not delinquent. Exactly what should be done in such cases? In the past all sorts of policies were developed to handle overlimit cases, and decisions regarding these cases are more and more frequently required as revolving credit and international travel continue to grow.

Another set of decisions involves the credit limit itself. What limit is to be assigned to each newly accepted applicant, and under what conditions in that limit to be raised or lowered? All too frequently in the past, credit limits assigned at application time were quite low, and changes in assigned limits were made reluctantly and were, consequently, rare.

Traditionally a decision was made regarding collateral. In former times, many finance companies decided on a case by case basis whether collateral was to be required. Exactly what the criteria were for making that decision were not well understood, and were usually not formal. Nowadays, with most credit in the revolving format, collateral is not an issue and the decision is less important.

In revolving credit accounts, the time comes when an account is to be considered for renewal. This is a decision to which scoring can be applied.

A area that is just beginning to get the attention is Authorizations. Enormous numbers of authorization inquiries are made daily around the world, and very large amounts of money are involved in the aggregate of these inquiries. Not only do the transactions involve large sums, but the process of authorization, the communications expense and the personnel involved, also require large investments. Improving the quality and speed of authorizations with procedures using scoring can result in very substantial cost reductions and lowered delinquencies.

Each time a credit decision comes up, the question is asked: Should a new credit bureau report be obtained? This is not always a simple matter. Credit reports are expensive, but a failure to get one on a decision that later turns out to produce a collection account can cause other problems for the people involved. It is well worth the trouble to consider the manner in which the decision to get or not to get a credit report is made and to seek to improve it by the application of any tools that are available.

Credit decisions are also often involved in the area of marketing, which is not usually considered a credit responsibility. In the past few years, many credit organizations have marketed various products through their billing systems. Finance company marketing is largely directed toward the promotion of further loans and credit lines. In many revolving card operations, other types of credit products are offered, such as open ended credit lines and loans based on second mortgages. In addition, many organizations are marketing merchandise and services not directly related to their credit operations.

Marketing mailing is expensive. Even stuffers in monthly statements are not free and special mailings are costly. Blanket mailings, as is commonly the case, send all the promotional material to everyone on the active file (and perhaps on some inactive files as well) with very little screening of delinquent accounts. Such mailings constitute a credit decision, since the merchandise or service will be delivered and the corresponding credit extended, regardless of the previous performance or the probability of satisfactory payment by the buyer.

In every one of the credit decisions enumerated above, the central question is: "What is the risk?". In every one of them, a properly constructed scoring system will provide the best estimate of the risk that is currently available and so can lead to the most profitable decision in each case.

I.1.3 Motivation for Change.

The replacement of a methodology that has served its purpose for centuries is not a trivial matter; the motivation must be compelling. Even when the motivation is strong, it is not necessarily the case that the transition from an earlier methodology to a new one will be simple or that it will be accepted without a struggle by the parties involved.

When the idea of replacing the traditional judgmental procedure for making credit decisions with scoring was first offered to the credit establishment it was not received with any conspicuous enthusiasm.

Far from it. Since the recommendation was coming from people with a background in mathematics, computers, and Operations Research, but definitely not credit, people in the credit field were more than a little hesitant. What could these scientific types possibly know about the complicated business of credit that would give them the right to say they had developed a way of making credit decisions that was better than the traditional methods that had proven successful for so long?

The criticisms offered by the credit establishment were not without some merit. The old ways had worked for a long time and the suggestion that they be replaced by something that added some numbers was not looked on with favor. The number of factors considered by an experienced credit analyst, along with the years of experience of these analysts, led the credit establishment to feel that no numerical procedure could possibly compete.

Sad to relate, this attitude still exists among many credit grantors, even some who have been using credit scoring successfully for years. However, despite the misgivings of many in the field, the pressure for the replacement of the traditional method has grown steadily over the past thirty years. Today it is a rash credit manager who will contend that he can do as well by judgment as he can with a scoring system.[1]

The pressures for change have come from various sources. The first, and possibly the most important, is the plain fact that the traditional methods are less effective than their champions believe.

A judgmental process is, by its very definition, unexplainable. The exact process through which a credit analyst, however "expert" he may be, reaches a conclusion is impossible to put into words; that is what "judgmental" means. As a result, the only way that credit judgment can be taught is in the apprentice mode. The apprentice sits at the feet of the master and tries to do things in the same way, with the master passing on to the student what experience he can verbalize. This is a costly process, and one that cannot be undertaken when the volume of decisions is large and the masters do not have the time to teach the students.

---

[1] It is worth noting that at least one scoring system manufacturer offers to compete in a carefully and fairly designed contest, and will gladly pay any losses incurred if scoring is shown to be inferior, provided that they be correspondingly compensated when scoring proves superior. No credit operation has ever accepted the challenge.

There are certain aspects of some credit decisions that can be reduced to a rule. Many credit operations decline credit to any applicant who has a record of a bankruptcy. Some elect to offer credit only to those with incomes over a certain level. Others require some minimum time at residence or employment. However, when these policy exclusions have been met, a decision must still be made, based on the available information, to grant or decline the requested credit. The number of factors is large.

A typical credit application may ask for as many as fifty separate pieces of information. Some applications may call for as many as 150 items. Many of the questions on an application can be answered with a Yes or a No, but most can have any of a variety of answers. If there are even as few as two possible answers to 50 questions, there are more than *one quadrillion* (that is, a 1 followed by 15 zeros) different combinations of information that might appear, and for each combination a decision may have to be reached.

Obviously, no one could possibly work out what decision is appropriate in each of such a vast number of cases. With traditional methods it is impossible for any individual to handle the immense diversity except in the most general of terms, which is why the apprentice can never exactly duplicate the decisions of his teacher. The student must learn what he can from the teacher and then apply what he has learned as best he can, trying as he goes to improve on his own performance.

Credit scoring, on the other hand, addresses exactly this diversity. Furthermore, it is fully explainable. All the factors that go into its construction are open to examination, all the methodology of computation can be reviewed to any depth that may be desired, and the way that the enormous number of alternatives have been considered is available for anyone to see.

Teaching about scoring does not require the apprentice mode, it can be done in classroom style and questions can be answered in detail and with all the necessary supporting information.

A second motivation for replacing individual judgment with a numerical process stems from the fact that individual analysts are human and subject to that particularly human characteristic of inconsistent behavior. Analysts have normal human feelings; on some days they feel better than on others, and on some days something can happen to make an analyst feel more, or perhaps less, tolerant of his fellows than usual. As a result, it is almost impossible for a human analyst to treat credit decisions in identical ways as time goes on. The application that is accepted on one day may easily be rejected on another. While analysts do their best to be consistent, they would be less than human if they were entirely so. Inconsistency is not a desirable characteristic in credit operations, so its removal by a more consistent procedure is attractive.

A corollary to the problem of inconsistency is that different analysts have slightly different views about what forms a sound credit decision. No two analysts will deliver exactly the same results when examining any substantial body of decisions. This non-uniformity of decision is undesirable, since a credit operation is generally interested in consistent behavior.

Obviously, a credit scoring table does not produce inconsistent results. The same facts will produce the same score every time (if accurately calculated), no matter who does it.

The inconsistency of individual judgment and the non-uniformity of decision among groups of credit analysts, undesirable enough on plain business grounds, is made even more serious by the laws and regulations of many jurisdictions regarding non-discrimination in credit. A rejected applicant, if he can find a similar (or even identical) application that has been accepted, presents a real legal hazard to any credit operation. The application of a numerical system that reaches the same conclusion on the same facts every time has the value of consistency and would appear to avoid a specific legal hazard.

While no credit grantor that I know of deliberately seeks to be discriminatory on any grounds, legal and regulatory developments over the past decade or so in the United States and in the United Kingdom have made discrimination on various grounds illegal. The first Equal Credit Opportunity Act (15 USC 1691 *et seq.*) was passed by the United States Congress in 1974 and was amended in 1976. This legislation directed the Federal Reserve Board to produce regulations necessary to enforce the Act, and the result was entitled Regulation B.[1] There has been activity in the United Kingdom to ensure that discrimination is not practiced, although this has been accomplished by voluntary action of credit grantors rather than by legislation. Since

[1] Copies of the legislation and of Regulation B, including the Official Staff Commentary of December 16, 1985, can be obtained from the nearest Federal Reserve Bank. Everyone in any phase of the credit industry in the U.S. should be fully aware of this legislation and of Regulation B.

scoring is a consistent and demonstrable process, many credit grantors were motivated to adopt scoring in part as a defense against a charge of discrimination.[1]

A further motivation for converting to numerical risk estimation arises from the difficulty in (in fact, the impossibility of) establishing close management control under a judgmental process. From time to time every credit department decides that it wants either to reduce the amount of credit or to increase it. Reductions in the amount of credit are called for when delinquencies grow to the point that management insists that they be reduced, and expansion of credit can be sought when management decides to broaden its business base, or for a variety of other reasons.

It is very hard for the management of a judgmental credit operation to reduce losses or to expand volume. In all too many cases, when losses begin to climb, management tells its credit division to "Tighten up on Credit". While this is a worthy exhortation, it doesn't tell the credit staff how to go about it. What management really would like to do is to tell the credit staff to reduce the risk it is taking by some specific amount. The very nature of a judgmental system precludes that form of communication; risk is not measured in any meaningful way and so cannot be adjusted.

At the other extreme, management has a similar problem when it wants to increase the amount of credit in its portfolio. Simply saying "Loosen up" is not a very helpful instruction. It is difficult, if not impossible, with judgmental procedures, to discuss anything other than extremes; it can shut the door almost completely or it can open it wide, but intermediate positions are hard to describe.

Various courses have been taken to get around these difficulties, and all of them have some value. For example, to "tighten up" on credit, a credit management might instruct its staff to require a full year of residence, rather than the six months that might have been the case in

---

[1]Oddly enough, there are two diametrically opposite views as to the value of credit scoring as a defense against a charge of discrimination. On one side are those who feel that a scoring system, demonstrably sound and empirically derived, is non-discriminatory almost by definition. The other side fears that a scoring system, presenting as it does the exact procedure for reaching a decision, exposes the user to the charge that some item in the scoring system, while not discriminatory on its face, is in fact a surrogate for some prohibited subject. By and large, the users of scoring as a clear demonstration of non-discrimination seem to be in the large majority, although no litigation has taken place to settle or even to discuss the subject.

the past. It might raise the minimum income required for acceptance, or disqualify some types of employment. In the process of "loosening" credit, the same procedures can be followed in reverse. While there is some merit to steps of this sort as a way of adjusting risk, none is as effective as the adjustment of the highest acceptable risk, in numeric form, that is only possible with scoring.

Hand in hand with the improvement in management control that is made possible with a scoring system is an improvement in communication, a strong motivation for change. Instead of having to say "Tighten up on credit", credit management can say, "Raise the lowest acceptable application score from 205 to 214". This is a very precise statement. As will be shown in Part II of this book, there is a direct relationship between score and risk. There is also a relationship between score and acceptance rate. Management will have, as part of the documentation of the scoring system, the table that relates score to risk and to acceptance rate. It can then adjust the lowest acceptable score so as to reduce the overall risk in the portfolio in a carefully measured way.

A second advantage of the statement: "Raise the lowest acceptable application score from 205 to 214" is that everyone understands it in exactly the same way. Each individual who is calculating scores and acting on the result will, after the announcement of the new lowest acceptable score, put those from 205 to 213, previously in the pile labeled "Recommend for Acceptance" into the one labeled "Recommend for Rejection". Furthermore, it is possible for supervisory management to ensure that its instructions are being carried out.

The end of the Second World War brought various changes in the way merchandise was sold. One of the most important changes was the encouragement of the use of credit by the larger merchandisers. Mail order companies such as Sears, Roebuck and Co., Montgomery Ward and Co., Inc., and J.C. Penney Co., Inc., developed credit portfolios of millions of customers. This meant that their application rates became enormous, in the tens of thousands of applications per month. Traditional methods were hard pressed to handle volumes of these dimensions. Retailers not involved primarily in mail order, such as the large department store chains, also increased their customer bases by using credit, again causing increased demand on the time of the credit analysts.

Beginning in about 1970 credit entered a phase of explosive growth in the United States and, a little later, in Western Europe. Many credit grantors switched from older forms of credit to revolving credit. Under this a customer had a continuing account that let him purchase up to some credit limit at any time without new documentation each time. At about the same time Master Charge® (later Master Card®) and Visa® went into full scale operation and enormous numbers of credit cards entered the market. In the expansion phase, these cards involved no annual fees, so that it was not uncommon for individuals to have a dozen or more cards. With application rates in the tens of thousands per month, it was no longer possible to spend the time needed for judgmental analysis and, in fact, there weren't enough analysts to go around.

There was some attempt by some card-issuing banks to draft credit analysts from the finance companies and to convert them to analysts of applications for revolving credit cards. This brought to light a problem that had already been recognized and solved by the developers of credit scoring systems; credit populations differ. The body of individuals who apply for credit from one credit grantor are never identical in their credit performance to those who apply to some other credit grantor, and they can be very different indeed. Consequently, if the same standards are applied in evaluating applications from two very different populations, the results can be far from desirable. If the criteria used in a high risk environment are applied to a lower risk case, the rejection rate will be far too high. Conversely, if the rules applied to a relatively low risk population are applied to a high risk one, delinquency losses will be unacceptable.

Having to tailor the decision criteria to each population presents a serious difficulty to the judgmental analyst. Such analysts have no way of measuring the underlying risk characteristics of any population, so when faced with a new population they have no alternative other than to apply their usual rules, with the possibility of making serious errors. This happened to some of the banks in their attempt to use finance company analysts to process applications for revolving credit cards.

With all their various deficiencies, traditional methods cannot be changed, no matter how strong the motivation. As long as all credit grantors were using the same methods, no one was very much better or worse than anyone else, so the general level of performance was considered acceptable. As soon as new tools appeared, however, it became possible for one credit grantor to achieve a level of performance dramatically better than its competitors, forcing the competition, however reluctant, at least to consider them. It is significant that no major credit grantor in the United States, to my knowledge, now operates without credit scoring as a major component of its decision process.

The change from traditional to analytical methods became possible when new tools became available after World War II. These new tools were computers and Operations Research.

Computers allow examination of large quantities of data in an efficient manner. In the 45 years following World War II computers became well integrated into American commercial life. From being curiosities in the hands of remote research organizations they became part of the every-day operations of American business, as well as in an astonishing number of American homes. This is rapidly becoming the case in Western Europe and in parts of Asia.

As early as 1970 credit grantors were well along in converting their billing operations to central computer files. In the years since then these central files have developed into enormously flexible sources of information for all sorts of commercial purposes including credit operations. From the early days when computers were the private domain of a few individuals trained in their use, they are now essential management tools that a large fraction of the labor force use in their daily work.

The development of Operations Research accompanied the development of computers in the commercial world[1] The term Operations Research is a broad and not very well defined expression covering the use of scientific methods to define and to solve problems. The field originated formally during World War II, but its potential for use beyond the sphere of military problems was obvious to many of its practitioners, who took its ideas into the universities and, gradually, into the world of business. Operations Research set out to express various business situations in mathematical terms and then to apply mathematical methods to make these situations more efficient, or less costly, or more profitable, or any mixture of these goals[2] The management of credit was one of the business situations ripe for study.

[1] In the United Kingdom this field is called "Operational Research", though I have never been able to find the origin of this difference.
[2] An example of the use of Operations Research that proved highly profitable is its application to warehouse management. In any complex warehouse, the single most difficult problem is to know when the level of inventory of any

A strong motivation for change is always the expectation of benefit, and in credit scoring the expected benefits were considerable. The principal anticipated benefit was better financial performance. Even the early credit scoring systems could show that, had they been in operation in the past, an organization using one would have experienced a reduction of an appreciable percentage in their delinquencies and charge-offs, with no loss of business. Alternatively, it could be shown that business could have been increased with no increase in losses. Either of these choices is most attractive and provided strong motivation for change.

Originally, the motivation for change was the prospect of financial benefit through application scoring. This motivation has been increased by the even greater prospect for financial benefits in the other areas of credit management: solicitations, re-issue, collections, over-limit action, credit limit setting and modification, and authorization as well as in marketing new products. Overall, the motivation is overwhelming.

I.2 History of Credit Scoring.

The history of credit scoring is short. There is no doubt that many credit managers attempted at various times in the past to reduce their procedure to some sort of numerical form, but until the development of the computers needed for the analysis of masses of data all of these attempts were fairly crude.

An exception was a pioneer in the field, Henry Wells, who was an executive of Spiegel Inc. During World War II he constructed a credit scoring system that was used at a time when many of his credit analysts were in the service and he needed tools that could be used by people with less experience. His work applied sound statistical techniques as far as that could be done without the computing power that is available today.

Several other individuals developed scoring methodologies during the 1950s but it was not until Fair, Isaac and Company entered the

item drops to the point when it should be re-ordered. If one waits too long, there is the chance of running out and the consequent annoyance, and possible defection, of the customer. If one orders too soon, the cost of maintaining the inventory becomes unacceptably high. If there are hundreds or thousands (and in some cases tens of thousands) of inventory items, this problem is critical to the survival of the organization. In the past thirty years enormous advances have been made in inventory theory to the general benefit of everyone concerned.

field that it began to become a significant factor in the credit industry.

The first task of these early developers, after devising the basic methodology that they were to use in building their scoring tables, was to gain the acceptance of the credit community. This was not a simple task, since traditional methods were deeply entrenched. The difficulty of assaulting the bastions of tradition was considerable; they did not succumb to the first approach. However, while there are still sceptics, the vast majority of credit in the United States is now granted by processes involving credit scoring to one degree or another.

The growth of the use of credit scoring has been a component of the change in American business brought about by increased awareness of the value of scientific analysis of problems of all sorts, not only those associated with credit. As a result, managements have become increasingly aware that technical methods must be evaluated carefully and that traditional methods will have to accept the challenge of new ideas and, if these new ideas prove to be more effective than the methods of the past, those past methods must disappear.

Managements have also become aware that competition is a broad term. Enterprises compete not only with pricing and variety and quality of merchandise, but in the manner in which they operate their businesses. Operations that are conducted more intelligently and with the use of sharper tools will drive to the wall those that disdain sharp tools and thoughtful practice.

Much of the initial effort in the process of introducing credit scoring was directed towards finance companies. This was because there were a lot of them and the problems of management and control were particularly acute in that area, in the view of the developers of scoring systems. The finance company world appeared to be a fertile field. Fertile or not, it was not a simple field to enter. The finance companies had well entrenched operations and recognized no pressing need for change. However, slowly but surely these companies began to consider the ideas of scoring and to adopt them, at least as a component of the credit decision process.

Not far behind the finance companies were the retailers. One of the first was Montgomery Ward and Co., Inc., then one of the country's major mail order firms. Wards, as it is commonly known, had millions of credit customers and a very large volume of applicants for credit accounts. In the mid-1960s each of the large branches had its own credit department, but the gradual installation of centralized billing computers made it possible for the company to consider centralized credit. Such centralization required a means for making credit decisions that was much faster than the traditional methods that were acceptable in the branch context. It was natural, therefore, for Wards to look into credit scoring, and when they did they entered the field in a big way. In the twenty years since Wards entered the field of analytical credit management, it developed into one of the most efficient (if not *the* most efficient) credit operation in the world.[1]

Other retailers quickly followed the example set by Wards. R. H. Macy and Co., Inc., Gimbel's, and Bloomingdale's, along with J. C. Penney and Co., Inc. and many others, adopted credit scoring as a basic management tool.

Credit cards were not as common in the 1960s as they are today, but even then large numbers of cards were issued by oil companies. In those days it was legal to mail unsolicited cards to individuals, and most oil companies did just that.[2] Even then, however, these same oil companies were considering more cautious credit procedures and they, too, began to investigate the possibilities of making credit decisions using scoring. Before long almost all of the major oil companies were using scoring as a basic tool.

Other organizations, such as those issuing the major Travel and Entertainment cards (American Express, Diners Club, and Carte Blanche), saw the possibilities of scoring quite early in their development, and the three major T&E cards all use scoring.

The major credit cards of today, Visa and Master Card, did not come into prominence until the early 1970s. When they arrived they came in with a bang. In the early days of Visa and what was then Master Charge, there was enormous competition and the cards were issued without a fee.[3] As a result, people applied for cards from many banks

---

[1] For reasons known only to the management of Wards, this entire operation was sold to the General Electric Credit Corporation in the late 1980s, as part of a complete re-structuring of the company.

[2] As the number of institutions offering credit cards increased, volume was developed by mailing unsolicited cards to large numbers of people. Many of these cards were stolen and their use caused serious problems to the individuals to whom they were supposed to have been issued, to say nothing of the litigation that resulted. In consequence, the mailing of unsolicited cards was prohibited by law.

[3] The Visa and Master Charge companies themselves did not issue cards or extend credit; they authorized individual banks and, later, other organizations

at the same time. This put a tremendous burden on these banks to process all these applications with reasonable speed. Traditional credit evaluation simply could not cope with the volume. This encouraged the major card issuers to consider using scoring as part of their procedure to speed up the decision process.

The wholesale granting of credit cards led, as could be expected, to very large losses by some of the issuers. These losses, in many ways more than the high volume, motivated credit grantors to look into credit scoring.

Other credit grantors followed along. Airlines began to use scoring in the issuance of their travel cards. Automobile financing companies, notably General Motors Acceptance Corporation, entered the field in 1979.[1] By the end of the 1970s credit scoring of applications for credit was a fully established process and almost all major credit grantors and many smaller ones employed it.

Early in the development of scoring questions arose to which there were no answers at the time. One was: How long does a scoring system last and how can we tell when to replace it? Another was: Since a scoring system is always based on the credit history of the organizations planning to use it, and since those organizations have rejected some fraction (in some cases a very large fraction) of the applicants, how can these rejected applications be taken into account?

A scoring system should be replaced when its performance degrades to a degree that, if replaced by a new system with performance equal to that of the original system at the time of its installation, the replacement will be profitable. In many cases, since there is now more data available, the replacement card will perform even better than the original.

The performance of a scoring system is measurable, as will be discussed in more detail in Part II of this book. One measure of performance is the difference between the average score of the Satisfactory accounts and the average score of the Unsatisfactory accounts. This measure of the performance of a scoring system is called its "divergence". The larger the divergence, the better. Over the years various

to do so; hence the large number of issuers and the consequent competition.

[1] GMAC, as this organization is known, is one of the largest consumer credit grantors in the world, if not the largest. In 1987 it extended consumer credit in the amount of close to $85,000,000,000.

procedures have been developed to measure the divergence of a system as time goes on after its installation.[1] Other methods, including comparing the continuing ability of the scoring system to rank order applicants, are available to examine the performance of a scoring system. Rank ordering can be affected when the population to which the scoring system is being applied is no longer statistically identical to the population upon which the original development of the scoring system was based. The analysis of the population that will lead to a conclusion as to whether or not the scoring system should be replaced is also discussed in Part II.

The second question, how to take into account the fact that applicants have been rejected in the past, proved to be a difficult problem. Several solutions have been developed and all are grouped for this discussion under the heading "Augmentation" in Section II.2.9. Accounts whose subsequent performance is known are *augmented* by rejected accounts whose performance is inferred by estimating how they would have behaved had they been accepted.

A third question that arose as far back as the 1960s was: In the case of revolving credit, where an account remains open for an extended period, and where the information given on the application loses its pertinence as time passes, how is that account's continued credit performance to be predicted? This question was answered by the development of what is called "Behavior Scoring".

Behavior scoring is a risk estimator similar to application scoring but uses for its development data the actual behavior of credit account holders (that is, the way in which the individual has used his credit, how much he has used, what, if any, delinquency history does he show, and other information available in the master billing record) rather than the information provided on the original application. While behavior scoring is not yet as widely used as application scoring, it is probable that it will become the dominant scoring procedure in the coming years. This subject will be discussed in Part III.

While scoring was being developed to a high level in the United States and Canada, most other countries were not aware of its usefulness. Some U.S. companies with subsidiaries abroad did attempt to

---

[1] There are at least a half a dozen different ways of measuring the performance of a scoring system. Each manufacturer will use the one that he prefers. In the end, all methods measure the ability of the scoring system to differentiate between satisfactory and unsatisfactory cases.

develop scoring systems for use overseas, but none of these attempts was particularly effective nor long-lasting. The Singer Company, at that time the world's best known maker of sewing machines, attempted to install scoring in Venezuela, the Philippines, and Mexico. While the scoring systems developed for these three cases were effective and would have been profitable to their owners, for a variety of reasons the systems were not maintained and were allowed to go out of use.

An executive of a British finance company who had previously worked with a scoring system in the United States, brought what may have been the first application credit scoring system to the United Kingdom. This scoring system was highly effective and led other credit executives in the British Isles to look into scoring. The U.K. is now the second largest user of scoring systems in the world. Since about 1980 many other countries in Western Europe, as well as countries in the Far East, including Australia, have entered the field. It is not too rash a forecast to predict that analytical techniques of credit management, including credit scoring, will be the norm around the world before the next century is very old.

Part II
Principles and Practice of Scoring

II.1 Getting Started.

II.1.1 Basic Ideas.

This part covers many of the nuts and bolts of the development of an application scoring system and its installation and operation, particularly those matters of concern to the user. Before we can get into these matters there are a few underlying ideas that need to be understood, and there are some conditions that must exist before any useful work can begin.

Fundamental to almost all human activity is the assumption that the near future will be something like the recent past. If this were not the case it would be difficult to get through the day. We expect the alarm clock to go off in the morning, just as it has on mornings in the past. We expect the milk in the refrigerator to be cold. We expect the bus to appear at its usual corner. We expect our place of employment to be there when we arrive. We expect our desks to be as we left them the day before.

When it comes to credit, we expect people as a group to behave more or less as they did in the past. We do not expect everyone to pay as agreed, but we do expect that, if other conditions remain the same, the delinquency rate will not be far different tomorrow from what it is today. We expect about the same number of applications to come in today as did yesterday, unless we have started a campaign for more applicants, in which case we would have made some prediction as to how many to expect. We would expect to accept about the same percentage of the applicants today as we did yesterday and we would expect about the same fraction of the acceptees to turn out to be unsatisfactory at some future date.

Both traditional credit evaluation and scoring base their predictions of the future on their knowledge of the past. Both methods compare today's applicants with experience with previous applicants, but they do it in very different ways.

In the judgmental mode the analyst compares the application that is before him (and the individual, if the application is made in person, as it is in many finance companies) with his experience in the past. If the new application appears to him to be more like those applications that he considered satisfactory in the past than it is to those applications that he considered *un*satisfactory in the past, he will accept the application. Since there are no absolute criteria that determine future satisfactory or unsatisfactory credit performance, all that remains is to try to associate a new case with the cases we have seen in the past.[1]

The same conditions surround scoring. Each new application is compared with the counted and structured information available about previous applicants embodied in the score table.

The one limitation that all analysts have is that they are confined to the information that is available to them; a credit application and frequently a credit bureau report. Analysts do not consider an applicant's favorite ice cream flavor, even though that might be an interesting indicator of performance, since it is not an available item of information. Over the years credit departments have developed applications that are astonishingly uniform. There are questions about the applicant's living arrangements, his job, his income, his assets, and his debts. While some applications ask more detailed questions than others, almost all ask something about these items.

Judgmental credit evaluators give weight to the information on applications according to their individual experience and training. For example, one analyst will give greater weight to *Time at Address* than *Time on Job*, while another will do the reverse. The relative importance that a judgmental analyst gives to the data on an application is highly personal and impossible to put into words. Scoring, operating on exactly the same information, determines by analysis the relative importance of the items on the application and sets them down in a score table. The analysis begins without any prejudice as to what is important and what is not. To start with, *all* the available information must be considered potentially valuable.[2]

---

[1] This is not something that is peculiar to credit. Almost every judgment we make is made on the basis of our understanding of earlier cases of a similar nature. When there is nothing we can use for comparison we have a serious difficulty. When Neil Armstrong landed on the moon he had only a guess as to what the surface would be like when he put his foot down, no one had any first hand experience to go on. Should an alien from another planet arrive on Earth, we would have no basis for deciding to give him a credit card or not, since we have never had the problem before.

[2] Information such as name and Social Security Number is needed for accounting purposes but is not included in the data for analysis.

While every item of information is of potential value (though not all are of *equal* value), we must keep in mind that they are not entirely independent of each other. Older people will, as a rule, have been on their jobs longer than younger people. Home owners will, as a rule, have higher incomes than renters. Single people will, as a rule, have fewer dependents than married people. In each case I have said "as a rule", since while these conditions apply broadly, there are many exceptions.

The exact manner in which these items interact is not readily apparent and is, in fact, very complex and difficult to determine. It is a source of much disagreement among judgmental credit analysts, since each has a view as to how these items interact, and these views can be very different among different analysts.

These differences will be particularly sharp among analysts from different backgrounds. An analyst who has worked exclusively with a small loan finance company will have views that are very different from those of one who has been making automobile loans with a rural bank. An important part of developing a scoring system is to address these interactions and take them fully into account.

The first step in any analytical approach to credit evaluation is to see precisely what the information on the application and the credit report tells us. The way to do this is to identify what information exists and then to count. This is done by assembling the applications of a body of accounts that we know have turned out to perform satisfactorily and another set of application documents of a body of accounts that we know have turned out to perform unsatisfactorily.[1]

We can now count how many Goods own homes and how many Bads own homes, how many Goods rent and how many Bads rent, and so on. We go on to count how many Goods are 18 years old, 19 years old, and so on up to some maximum, and we do the same for the Bads. We carry out this process of counting for *every one* of the items of information that was available to the analysts (from whatever source) at the time they made their decisions. This is done without any pre-judgment as to what will turn out to be important and what will not, since to begin with we disclaim any certain knowledge as to what is important.

[1] It has become the custom of the credit scoring industry to describe applicants whose accounts have performed in a satisfactory manner as "Good" and those that have not as "Bad". This is a convenient shorthand and I will use it from here on.

This counting procedure is always most revealing. While every credit analyst can make statements like: "There are many, many more home owners than renters in our customer base", only very few can tell you even approximately what fraction are owners and what fraction are renters. Furthermore, he will usually contend that home owners are "better risks" than renters, but he has no way of telling you how much better risks they are. The counting process answers these questions. It will show the percentage of Good accounts that belong to home-owners and the percentage of Bad accounts of home owners and the corresponding percentages for the renters. If we assembled a sample of 1,000 Goods and 1,000 Bads, the results might look like the numbers in Figure 2.[1]

Figure 2

Hypothetical Example of Counts and Percentages of Owners and Renters				
	Goods		Bads	
	Nr.	%	Nr.	%
Own	600	60%	200	20%
Rent	300	30%	700	70%
Other	100	10%	100	10%

From these percentages we can calculate the "odds to be Good", as shown in Figure 3, by dividing the percent Goods by the percent Bads for each attribute. Figure 3 shows that, in this simplified example, and *if no other information is available*, the odds are three to one that a home owner will turn out to be Good, while the odds for a renter are only 3/7 or .43 to 1 to be Good. Clearly, the owners are to be preferred as risks.[2] These are called the Information Odds.

Now let us add another item of information, similarly simplified and exaggerated in the interest of simplicity. Consider the information regarding *Age*, as displayed as percentage information in Figure 4.

---

[1] The figures in this table and all the others in this book are illustrative only. Some been rounded to make it easy to do arithmetic with them.

[2] In this simple case the same result would be reached by dividing the *number* of Goods by the *number* of Bads, rather than using the percentages, but in most cases there are not equal numbers of Goods and Bads so that it is easier to work with the percentages.

Figure 3

Hypothetical Example of Odds to be Good			
	Percent Goods	Percent Bads	Odds to be Good
Own	60%	20%	3/1
Rent	30%	70%	3/7 or .43/1
Other	10%	10%	1/1

Figure 4

Hypothetical Example of Age Distribution in Percentages			
Age	Percent Goods	Percent Bads	Odds to be Good
Under 30	10%	40%	1/4 or .25/1
30 - 39	20%	40%	1/2 or .5/1
40 - 49	30%	10%	3/1
50 and Over	40%	10%	4/1

Statistical theory tells us that if phenomena, such as *Type of Residence* and *Age*, are independent, the odds can be calculated by multiplying the odds for the individual cases.[1] For example, from Figures 3 and 4, we see that a 55 year old home owner, if age and home ownership are independent, has odds of 4/1 times 3/1 or 12/1 of proving to be a Good account. This means that of 13 applicants in the historical record of this hypothetical lender who were 55 years old and who owned homes, 12 turned out well and one turned out badly.

The same Figures show that a 21 year old renter had odds of only 1/4 times 3/7 or 3/28 or about 1 chance in 9 to prove to be good. While these figures show that a young renter has proved a greater risk than an older home owner, which can hardly be a surprise, it should also be noted that the odds get a lot closer if the young person owns a home (3 to 4) and the older is a renter (12 to 7). On the assumption that the

---

[1]*Independence* means that there is no degree of association of any type between two characteristics. In the real world, in practically every case there is some degree of association between almost any two characteristics. In the case of Home Ownership and Age the association is usually quite strong; most young people cannot afford to own homes.

future will be like the past, these odds to be Good can be used as predictors of future risks.

Tables similar to those if Figures 2, 3, and 4 are made for every item that can be determined from the application and the credit report (if one was obtained), as will be discussed more fully below in the Section II.2.7, entitled "Initial Enumeration". Examination of the sample counts usually proves revealing of facts about the customer population that were unknown or unsuspected by management. This in itself would make the effort worth while, but it is only an early step in the process of scoring table development.

II.1.2 Total Odds, Information Odds, and Population Odds.

The foregoing discussion of odds considered only the Information Odds; that portion of the Odds to be Good that can be calculated from the information we can discover about applicants. That is only part of the story. The total amount of information that can be determined, and consequently the Total Odds to be Good, depends not only on the percentages of the applicant population that have different attributes but on the nature of the population itself. Mathematically, this is stated as follows:

Total Odds to be Good = Information Odds x Population Odds[1]

The Population Odds means the overall odds that would be shown if all applicants to a particular credit grantor had been granted credit. If such a thing were to happen, over time it would develop that most of the accounts would pay in an acceptable manner while some would not. The ratio of the Goods to the Bads, without considering any of the information that can be acquired about applicants, is the Population Odds. Obviously, this procedure is rarely, if ever, followed, since it would result in an unacceptably large number of Bad accounts going on the books. However, there are ways to estimate the Population Odds and these will be discussed under the heading "Augmentation" in Section II.2.9, The Calculation of Score Points.

While it is useful to know the Total Odds presented by any particular applicant for credit, it is not essential to the process of scoring or to the mathematics of scoring system development. The development of

---

[1] The mathematical derivation of this relationship is beyond the scope of this book, but it is available is various statistical texts that treat Baysean statistics. In the examples in Section II.1.1 the Population Odds were set to 1/1.

a scoring system exhausts, as best it can, the information made available by applicants so that a relative scale of odds can be established. This means that it is possible to rank order all applicants starting with those with the best Information Odds to be Good down to those with the worst. The Population Odds, if known or inferred, when multiplied by the Information Odds for each case, will establish the Total Odds, but this will not change the rank order. Scoring systems can be operated without ever estimating the Population Odds. In fact, when scoring systems were first developed there was no known way to estimate the Population Odds; it was several years after scoring systems began to be widely used that the mathematics of the inference of the Population Odds was developed.

At first thought it might be supposed that all credit populations are very much the same and that their Population Odds would all be equal or very close. I was surprised to learn, as my experience with scoring systems grew, and as the methods of estimating Population Odds made it possible for us to find out, that there is a surprisingly large range to these figures. While most populations seem to lie between 10-to-1 to 20-to-1, I have seen Population Odds as low as 1-to-1 and as high as 125-to-1.

A second thought suggests that a wide range in Population Odds is not as unexpected as it might appear. People who are excellent credit risks can get credit from institutions with moderate interest rates while individuals who are less satisfactory risks frequently must seek credit from institutions that charge a higher interest rate. The groups that go to the two different types of lenders are different in their overall performance.

II.1.3 Suitable Populations.

The development of a statistically sound credit scoring table depends on counting the frequency of occurrence of many items of information about Good and Bad accounts. Since credit portfolios vary in size from a few thousands of accounts to many millions, samples are used. Trying to deal with all the documents of a very large credit portfolio is a hopeless task, but sampling methods have been shown to be effective in many areas of statistical research, and they are entirely valid here.

There is no magic number for the "best" size of a sample, but long practice has demonstrated that if a total of 1500 Good and 1500 Bad accounts can be collected for analysis, the result will be effective and robust.[1] The limiting factor here is the number of Bad accounts that can be assembled. While at first glance every credit manager is sure he has available all too many Bad accounts, when we get down to collecting them we frequently find there are not as many as was first thought. In order to benefit most from the idea that "the near future will be like the recent past", the more recent the interval that we use for "the past" the more similar it will be to the future. If we can collect a sample of 1500 Bad accounts from accounts that went on the books in the past 12 to 24 months, we can make a more effective scoring table than if we spread out the bad accounts over the previous 3, 4, or 5 years.

It is also helpful if the sample on which the scoring table is to be based has been stable and homogeneous for the period from which the Bad and Good accounts are to be selected for analysis. By *stability* I mean that the enterprise offering the credit has been in the same business and operating in more or less the same way over the interval of interest.

If, over the past year or so, the enterprise has undertaken dramatic expansion programs, especially expansion into segments of the population not previously served, or expansion into a new geographical area, resulting in a short term flood (or even several bursts) of applications from new parts of the population, the nature of the Good and Bad accounts will show a broader range of attributes than would be the case if the served population had been unchanged.

By *homogeneity* I mean that the population of interest has been offered only one credit product over the interval of interest. A population served only by, say, Master Card is better for the purposes of the development of a scoring system than, say, a population offered both Master Card and automobile loans. A mixture of secured and unsecured credit products is less satisfactory as a base for a scoring system than is a population using either secured or unsecured credit alone.

While a population with both stability and homogeneity is highly desirable, it is not always possible to provide one. In such cases

---

[1] By "robust" I mean that the scoring table will perform as expected for a reasonable length of time, typically between one and five years. Presidential elections in the United States have been predicted with accuracy (except in the case of the unfortunate Alf Landon) based on samples of around 1000 individuals nationwide.

considerable thought is called for to decide whether to proceed. If the population has been highly volatile, or if there has been a lack of homogeneity due to the variety of credit products offered, consideration should be given to selecting only one product so as to limit the population of interest, or waiting for some interval to allow the effect of population variation to settle down. In very small credit operations, where getting 1500 Bad accounts from the past two years is hard under any conditions, a scoring system can still be produced, but its power may be lower than would have been possible with a more stable or a more homogeneous population.[1]

An obvious condition that must be met if a scoring system is to be developed is that information must be available. A prospective scoring system user must must be able to identify the sample of 1500 Good and 1500 Bad accounts that are to be examined, and must be able to locate and assemble the original applications for all those accounts along with the credit bureau reports in every case where one was obtained.

This requirement is fairly easy to satisfy in the United States, since by law credit grantors are required to retain all application information for at least 25 months, including (and especially) records of those that were turned down. In countries where no such retention is required by law, the location and collection of the necessary raw data may be difficult or, in some cases, impossible. Any credit grantor who is even considering the development of a credit scoring system should begin immediately to retain all credit application information so that when the time comes to proceed with a scoring system the data will be available.

II.2 Scoring System Development.

II.2.1 The Liaison Team.

Now that the basic ideas have been presented, we need next to establish a liaison team, select the appropriate population, and define Good and Bad performance. When these things are done we are ready to start building an application scoring system.

---

[1] If we use, for the sake of this discussion, the figure of 6% for the fraction of Bads to be found in a portfolio, and if 1500 Bads are what is sought, then the enterprise must have accepted no fewer than 25,000 applications over the interval of interest, usually two to two and one half years. If the rejection rate is, say, 50%, then there must have been 50,000 applications in that interval.

First, the liaison team. A team must be set up to act as the interface between the user organization and the scoring system manufacturer. It would be hard to overestimate the importance of the liaison team throughout the development and installation of the system, as well as in the initial stages of operation. Even for experienced users of scoring systems, each system has its own little peculiarities that must be thoroughly understood by everyone concerned, both inside the organization and in the manufacturing company.[1]

The liaison team will be responsible for the initial discussions with the manufacturer so that everyone is clear regarding the population to be served by the system, the definitions of Good and Bad accounts, and the time frame for the development and delivery of the system. From then on the liaison team will be an integral part of almost every step in the process, except for the actual process of calculating score points, and even there they will have something to contribute.

An important task of the liaison team is to prepare management to address the decisions that must be made what a scoring system is installed. These should be brought up early in the course of system development to make the installation as smooth as possible. Installation is discussed in Section II.3.

The liaison team must be selected with these duties in mind. At least one member of the team, preferably the team leader, should be senior enough to make decisions on most matters without delaying production. He should be (or become) sufficiently familiar with scoring to know what is coming next and what part he will need to play.

Ideally, a member of the liaison team comes from the data processing and billing department of the user organization, and is someone who can get action from the data processing group when it is needed. This individual must also communicate to the data processing group whatever information it will need to help the organization integrate scoring into its regular operations when it is delivered.

Since various United States laws, such as the Equal Credit Opportunity Act and the Fair Credit Reporting Act, have impact on the manner in which credit scoring is developed and used, it is advisable

---

[1] Even if you are planning to make your own scoring system, the functions carried out by the liaison team still need to be performed. Everyone involved in scoring, directly or indirectly, either in its manufacture or its subsequent use needs to be kept informed as to what is happening and what part they must play.

to have a representative of the legal department on the liaison team. In other countries scoring may have legal ramifications as well, so it is useful to include the legal department in any plans in this area.

It is this liaison team, and particularly its leader, that will be responsible for the training of the people who will be connected with the delivered scoring system as well as for the education of the management people who must make certain decisions with regard to the system and who will evaluate its performance as time goes along. All the people who will work with the scoring system must be completely familiar with it, with how it was developed, and with how it is to be used to achieve maximum benefit. This includes the most junior of clerks through the most senior of managers in the credit department (as well as the other management people who will be responsible at higher levels).

It is all too often the case that the scoring system is considered a minor affair unworthy of the attention of anyone outside the development team. When this is the corporate view, there is always a moment of shock when management realizes how great an impact the scoring system is having on the overall credit portfolio. Then there is a great scramble to learn what should have been learned at the beginning; much time and benefit having been thrown away.

II.2.2 The population.

Almost the first task of the liaison group (and the management of the user organization) will be to select the precise population on which the scoring system is to be operated and, consequently, the source for all of the historical data that will be needed for its development. As mentioned earlier, the more stable the population and the fewer the credit products offered to that population, the better, from the point of view of scoring system construction.

If a population can be found that uses only a single credit product and has not undergone any large scale shifts in membership type, and if that population has sufficient history to provide the necessary documents regarding 1,500 Good and 1,500 Bad accounts, many complications that frequently arise will be avoided.

As a rule of thumb, any population that can supply the necessary historical information over a one or two or even three year history will provide the grounds for a profitable application scoring system.[1] If, for example, a bank had a body of secured loans and a body of unsecured loans and each was sufficient to provide the needed information, that bank would do well to buy two systems, even though the cost would be higher, than to put the populations together and make one system to cover them both. The predictive power of each of the separate systems would almost certainly be sufficiently greater than the predictive power of a system built on the joint population that they would produce benefits that would more than offset the increase in cost.

If there are two or more candidate populations, and if the organization is new to the idea of scoring, then it probably makes sense to work on that population where the application and bureau information are in the best shape. However, the user organization itself may have strong views on which is the most important population and those views should govern unless someone can make a convincing case to the contrary.

II.2.3 Definitions of Good and Bad accounts.

We have used the terms Good and Bad accounts frequently up to this point without getting specific about what a Good account is and what a Bad account is. In theory, a Good account is one that you are glad you took and a Bad account is one that you are sorry that you took. That may be true but it isn't very helpful. Good and Bad accounts must be defined in terms that are sufficiently precise so that observers will all come to the same conclusions about each. This means that it is easiest if accounts are defined in terms of their manner of performance.[2] A Good account in a revolving credit operation might be someone whose billing account shows:

1. On the books for a minimum of 10 months.
2. Activity in six of the most recent 10 months.
3. Purchases of more than $50 in at least three of the past 24 months.
4. Not more than once 30 days delinquent in the past 24 months.

---

[1] While I have not seen this proved mathematically, I have seen it demonstrated in several thousand actual cases, in none of which was any system defect detected due to the size of the development sample.

[2] Whether an account is Good or Bad is determined entirely from its performance *once accepted*. No part of the definition includes information on the application or the credit bureau report.

These conditions take note of the fact that until someone has been on the books for some interval, it is not possible to know if you are happy with them or not. The activity requirement and the requirement that some minimum dollar level be reached further restrict the allowable candidates by removing those whose activity is too low to be meaningful or whose dollar involvement is minimal. Obviously, every management will have its own views on these sorts of conditions, as they will have on the definition of a Bad account.

A Bad account in a revolving charge case is a little more difficult to describe, but the following might be adequate definitions:

Delinquent for 90 days or more at any time with an outstanding undisputed balance of $50 or more.

or

Delinquent three times for 60 days in the past 12 months with an outstanding undisputed balance on each occasion of $50 or more.

or

Bankrupt while account was open.

With definitions of this type it is possible to write a computer program to scan a billing file and identify all those who qualify in either category. There are some accounts that do not fall into either group; newly acquired accounts, for example, accounts 60 days delinquent once or even twice at some time in the past, and so on. These are indeterminate accounts. The account that has been 60 days delinquent once is not so clear, but it will usually be agreed that there is not enough information for the qualitative decision: Are we glad we saw this person or are we not? Some number of indeterminate accounts will develop in every case.

II.2.4 Acceptance Rate.

An additional chore that the liaison team should undertake as early as possible, since it is not always a simple matter, is to determine what fraction of applications over the past two or three years (and possibly, year by year) have been accepted. This is a figure that is used later during the construction of the scoring system when estimating the nature of the entire population of applicants. The acceptance rate is not always immediately available and may need some digging to find. Many organizations keep track of the acceptance rate by maintaining running records of the numbers of accounts accepted and rejected, but at worst it will require someone to hand count the accepted and the rejected applications.

II.2.5 Acquisition of sample data.

We are now ready to begin to develop the scoring system. The first tangible step is the collection of the sample data. In a portfolio of one million accounts of which six percent are Bad, and an indeterminate population of ten percent, there are 840,000 Good accounts and 60,000 Bad accounts. If accounts remain active, on the average, for six years, then only one third of each group, more or less, can be expected to have come on the books in the past two years, leaving possible candidates at around 280,000 Good and 20,000 Bads.

The full figure of 1,500 Good and 1,500 Bad sample accounts will not always be used in developing the scoring system. If 1,000 complete sets of documents can be acquired for the Goods and for the Bads, a fully satisfactory scoring system will result. In fact, this number is frequently about what is used in practice, since usually some sets of documents (perhaps as many as a couple of hundred) will prove either to have been selected in error or to be insufficiently complete to be useful. In addition, between 200 and 300 accounts are frequently set aside to be used to test the scoring system when it is completed, a procedure called "validation", which is described under the heading "Development Time Validation" in Section II.4, Operation.

Samples from a master billing file. When a master billing file is available, the selection of the members of the sample is straightforward. The first step is to provide the manufacturers with a copy of the most recent master billing tape. If closed accounts are kept on a separate tape, that will also be needed, as will any other special purpose tapes that contain account records covering the most recent three or four years.

At this point each manufacturer will follow its own procedures, but in general the task is to go through all of the pertinent records and to identify (and mark) all Good and all Bad accounts, according to the definitions that have been agreed upon, and to count the total of each![1]

[1] Throughout this book I use terminology and refer to methodology that I learned as an employee of Fair, Isaac and Company, Inc. Every manufacturer of scoring systems has its own methods for dealing with the various problems

If the first pass through the tape files shows that there are 280,000 Good accounts and 20,000 Bad accounts, as we calculated in the example given above, then for the sample we need every 187th Good record and every 13th Bad record.

If we can be assured that the account numbers were assigned in time sequence, that is, as the applications were received and with no component of geography or commodity or any other distinguishing mark, then literally taking every 187th Good and every 13th Bad on the file will identify the desired accounts. A list is produced of the chosen accounts, including the name, the account number, and whether that account is Good or Bad. Additional information may be added if it is felt that it would help in locating the associated documents.

The next step is to assemble, based on the list of desired accounts, the application form and any credit bureau report for each name on the list. Ledger information is not necessary, since we already know if each account is Good or Bad; what we are interested in now is the body of application time information. In most cases the user organization assembles the required papers, since it is more familiar with its own files than is any outsider, and its efforts will be less disruptive than an intrusion from outside.

The requirement in the United States that application information be kept for a minimum of 25 months makes the assembly of application information much less complicated than it used to be. In the "good old days", if the originals had not been thrown away, they were usually in some dismal warehouse that took considerable effort to penetrate. In countries where document retention is not required, that may still be the case. Any organization contemplating the development of an application scoring system should begin to retain its information as soon as possible so that it will be ready when the time comes.

In this section I introduced the assumption, rather casually, that about six percent of the accounts were Bad. However, this is not a statistic we know until after we have examined the master file and counted the involved in the production, installation, and operation of credit scoring systems, and each may use its own terminology. Each time a method is discussed or a term used, the reader should keep in mind that other manufacturers may have methods that differ to a greater or lesser extent as well as different terms. It should also be remembered that all manufacturers face the same overall problems and the solutions described here are intended only to show that solutions exist.

exact number of Good and Bad accounts in the whole portfolio. It is only then that we can calculate this number, which is known as the Bad Rate. It is needed later in the process of developing the scoring system.

Samples when there is no master billing file. This is a situation that does not arise as often today as it did in the past, at least in the United States. It may still come up in some other countries, so it is worth a word or two.

When there is no master billing file, as can happen with organizations with many locations, where several (and perhaps all) have a billing and a credit function, there is no easy and convenient way of identifying the accounts that should compose the sample. There is nothing for it but to go to the branches and look through the files. In a finance company with, perhaps, 500 or even 1,000 or more branches, it is not feasible to visit them all, so the usual course is to select about ten percent of the branches, carefully chosen to be as representative of the entire organization as possible.

The liaison team should take a part in this selection, since they are better placed to know, or to find out, if any of the branches has special peculiarities that would bar it as a true representative of the organization and of the area in which it is located. Next, a schedule should be set up for visiting the branches, and these branches should be notified and told what is about to happen.

Before visiting the branches, the scoring system manufacturer and the liaison team will decide, from the total number of accounts in each of the selected branches, how many Good and how many Bad account records they want from each. Allowance will be made to over-sample slightly, since there may be branches where a full sample cannot be acquired, for one reason or another.

On visiting a branch, the sample takers will ask to see the current delinquent files and will locate as many Bads as they can.[1] They will also look for Bads in the closed account file. They will identify the number they are seeking and then try to find the original application forms and their associated credit bureau reports in those cases where one was obtained.

---

[1] In most cases the scoring system manufacturer will insist on taking the sample with its own staff, since they are usually experienced in the process and are aware of its importance. It is helpful if the user sends a representative on the sample gathering tour.

It will usually not be possible to remove the original documents from the branch, so that some arrangement must be made either to micro-film the documents or to run them through some sort of document copier. Nowadays copying machines are readily available in the United States, but in countries outside North America some thought should be given, well in advance, as to how the documents are to be copied.

As noted earlier, one by-product of the search of a Master Billing file is the determination of the Bad Rate: the fraction of the accounts that are Bad. If there is no Master Billing file, the determination of the Bad Rate is not so simple. If the organization is widely dispersed, it may be necessary to poll the individual offices and ask them to report the total number of Good accounts and the total number of Bad accounts that they have on their books.

The use of rejected applications. Up to this point we have discussed only the applications that turned into Good or Bad accounts. How-ever, there is another body of applications that requires consideration; the applications that were rejected because they were thought to be too risky.

The scoring system to be developed is intended to be applied to the entire population through the door, not only to those that the previous system would have approved. If a scoring system is constructed using only applications accepted by the methods that are to be replaced, it will have built into it the overall effect of these old methods.

To avoid this pitfall, it is necessary to make an inference as to how the rejected applicants would have performed, Good or Bad, had they been accepted. This process of inference, called Augmentation, is discussed in Section II.2.9, below. By making this inference, and adding to the known Goods and Bads the inferred Goods and Bads from the rejected applicants, we can construct our best estimate of the true nature of the entire population served by that particular credit grantor. The scoring system built on this full population will better serve the future population through that user's set of doors.

To round out the complete sample, the only thing that remains is to assemble from 750 to 1,000 rejected applications, with their bureau reports, if acquired. Since retention is required in the U.S., their assembly should cause no trouble. However, attention should be paid to make sure that the rejected sample does not contain applications that were declined on the grounds of corporate policy. Some organizations turn down previous bankrupts, regardless of their present condition; no judgment is exercised, the application is turned down. Similarly, applications from outside the geography covered by the organization are usually declined, and these, too, should not be in the sample of the rejects. Any other policy declines should be detected and removed from the sample.

With the 1,500 Good applications, the 1,500 Bad applications, and the 1,000 or so Rejected applications, with any credit bureau reports that were acquired, the sample is complete and we can go to the next step in the development of the application scoring system.

II.2.6 Coding.

The process of preparing the information on the credit applications and their associated credit bureau reports to be put into computer usable form is called Coding.

The first step in coding is to find out how many different forms are present. Most organizations are confident that they have only one application form, but frequently variants appear. Sometimes these variants are very different and carry substantially different information. For example, there is a great difference between a question on Housing that provides two check boxes, one for Own and one for Rent, and one that is accompanied by a blank that is filled in by the applicant in whatever way each particular applicant happens to think is wanted. Similarly, there can be a great difference in the result if there is a large space in which to respond to the request for "Other credit accounts" or if there are only a couple of short lines.

It is helpful to start with the current application form and to see how many of the items that appear on that form can be extracted from the various other application forms that appear in the sample.[1]

Characteristics. The next step in preparing the sample data for analysis is to identify of all of the items of information that can be extracted from the applications and credit bureau reports in the sample

---

[1] It is wise to look forward, as well. On one occasion, one of my colleagues delivered a scoring system only to discover that, unbeknownst to anyone in the credit department, the marketing department, seeking to expand the customer base by making it easier to apply, had produced a new application form containing only one or two of the items that were components of the scoring system. Liaison teams, take note.

data. To be useful, the items identified must be among whose that will be on the application form that will be in use when the scoring system goes into effect. These items, usually in the form of questions on the application and of entries in credit bureau reports, are called *Characteristics*.

Applications for credit come in many shapes and sizes. As a rule, those for loans from banks and finance companies appear to be considerably more complicated than those for credit cards, but this is changing gradually in the direction of simplification. However, even when two applications appear to be very different at first sight, examination may show that there is a good deal of similarity in the information that is asked for.[1]

Figure 5 shows the lists of Characteristics identified on three different U.S. applications, one from an organization offering sales finance loans, and two from companies offering Visa and Master Cards. Note that twelve of the Characteristics are common to all three, while each has items not asked for by the others.

Credit grantors that make repeated loans to the same individuals usually note on the application the performance of their borrowers on the previous or current loans. Some of the types of Characteristics that refer to previous borrowing are shown in Figure 6.

Application forms outside of North America are changing rapidly as lenders become familiar with the problems of risk estimation and the information that such estimation requires. While most credit grantors, wherever they may be located, ask such things as Age of Applicant, Occupation, Time at Address, Time with Employer, Type of Residence, outside the U.S. many other questions are asked.

In the United Kingdom, in addition to most of the questions asked on U.S. applications, there are questions regarding the length of time the applicant has had the same occupation, regardless of the number of jobs he may have had. Frequently the lender requests a recommendation from the banker where the applicant has an account. In addition, there is a formal categorization of housing that divides housing into such groupings as Agricultural, Higher Income, Poor Quality, Multi-Racial, High-Status Non-Family, Affluent Suburban, and so on.

---

[1]This is true for applications in the United States and Canada. In most of the rest of the world credit and applications for it are quite new and are still in the process of development.

Figure 5

		On Sales Finance Application	On Visa/MC Application - I	On Visa/MC Application - II
	Comparison of Characteristics From Three Applications			
1	Bank Card / T&E Card Reference	X	X	X
2	Zip Code	X	X	X
3	Time At Present Address	X	X	X
4	Time at Previous Address	X	X	X
5	Residential Status	X	X	X
6	Occupation	X	X	X
7	Time With Employer	X	X	X
8	Applicant's Monthly Salary	X	X	X
9	Other Income	X	X	X
10	Checking Account Reference	X	X	X
11	Savings Account Reference	X	X	X
12	Bank Card / T&E Card Reference	X	X	X
13	Department Store Card Reference	X	X	X
14	Number of Dependents	X	X	
15	Bank Loan Reference	X	X	
16	Finance Co. Loan Reference	X	X	
17	Total Monthly Payments	X	X	
18	Total Assets	X		
19	Total Dollars Owed	X		
20	Age of Automobile	X		
21	Telephone		X	
22	Oil Company Reference		X	
23	Highest Educational Level			X

Figure 6

	Typical Characteristics of New, Current, or Former Borrowers
1	Borrower Type - New, Current, or Former
2	Dealt With For YY Years
3	Time Since Last Loan
4	Amount of Last Loan
5	Balance Due on Previous Loan
6	Highest Delinquency on Last Loan

In Germany the applicant is asked if he has yet completed his military obligation. They also frequently ask, as do most non-U.S. lenders, for marital status and sex. Italian lenders frequently ask for province of birth and whether the marital contract calls for community property. In France and Belgium an applicant is frequently asked for his country of origin, language, and the length of time he has been in the country.

In Japan a great deal of importance is given to the applicant's employer; whether that employer is publicly traded, the size of its capitalization, and number of its employees. In addition, since a special compensation payment, loosely called a bonus, is paid to Japanese workers twice a year, there is frequently a question about the size of the most recent bonuses and the ratio of the bonus to the standard monthly wage. A particularly endearing question that sometimes shows up is "What is the Applicant's Hobby", but I have no information about its value as a predictor of future credit performance.

As usual, Japanese applications ask for the age of the applicant, but some special logic has to be built into the data-gathering program since many older or more traditional Japanese give their age in terms of a number of years since the death of an Emperor. These are only a few examples of differences between U.S. applications and those used in other countries. Many other examples will appear when individual cases are examined.

Credit Bureau Characteristics. In the United States there are currently several automated credit bureaus and many independent bureaus. Many large creditors serve extended areas, including some that are nationwide in their coverage, and these creditors receive reports from several, if not all, of the automated bureaus as well as from some of the independents. The types of Characteristics that are commonly developed from credit bureau reports are shown in Figure 7.

Outside the United States and Canada credit bureaus are not common. They are being developed in Europe and Japan, but they are only starting in most other countries. In the United Kingdom credit reporting is well advanced, though some of the information maintained would appear strange to a U.S. bureau. For example, a credit report can contain derogatory information about individuals living at the address (and sometimes also the former address) of the applicant, even if the name of the individual to whom the report refers is not the same as that of the applicant. Credit reports in the U.K. sometimes

Figure 7

	Typical Characteristics Developed from Credit Bureau Reports
1	Credit Bureau Used
2	Time Since First Credit Entry
3	Number of Satisfactory Reports
4	Number of Minor Derogatory Reports
5	Number of Major Derogatory Reports
6	Number of Inquiries

cover credit experience in the neighborhood in which the applicant lives.

Credit grantors outside the United States are not under all of the restrictions imposed on U.S. lenders by various laws and regulations.★ Under the Equal Credit Opportunity Act it is unlawful in the United States to discriminate based on Race, Color, Religion, National Origin, Sex, Marital Status, or Age. As a result, no questions on any of these items is asked on any U.S. application except in a few special cases specifically permitted under the law. Countries other than the United States are under no such restrictions, so that questions on all of these items can appear on applications.

Many scoring systems use geographic indicators such as postal code or zip code. Outside the U.S. there is no problem with postal codes and they are usually found to be useful. In the U.S., however, there is still some concern that the use of zip code might result in discrimination if zip codes that develop low scores were to be shown to be inhabited predominantly by any group that is protected by law against discrimination. As a result, some manufacturers prefer to avoid zip codes or to use only the first two or three digits.

Attributes. The answers given to questions on the application, and the entries on the credit report are known as *Attributes*. For example, *Own* is an Attribute of the Characteristic, *Do you own or rent your home?* Similarly, *26* is an Attribute of the Characteristic, *Age*. The scoring system manufacturer has to determine just what Attributes associate with each of the Characteristics. The liaison team will have a part in this, since the management of the user must, in the end, approve of the Characteristics that are to be eligible for inclusion in the final scoring system and will also approve the Attributes that will be considered for each of the Characteristics. Determining suitable Attributes is not always as simple as it looks. On one occasion I was involved in the development of a scoring system from an application that presented the applicant with a blank space for *Type of Residence*. We reported to management that the sample had shown that there were statistically meaningful numbers in each of the ten Attributes for the Characteristic, as shown in Figure 8.

Figure 8

Possible Attributes for Characteristic:*Type of Residence*	
1	Own, Free and Clear
2	Own, Mortgage
3	Own, Land Contract
4	Rent, Unfurnished
5	Rent, Furnished
6	Dormitory
7	Barracks
8	Mobile Home, Small
9	Mobile Home, Large
10	Other

Compare this with the three examples of *Residential Status* referred to in Figure 5. The Sales finance lender asked only for *Own* or *Rent*, while the first Visa-Master Card issuer had check boxes for *Own*, *Rent*, or *Other*. The second Visa-Master Card issuer called for one of the following: *Own Home, Own Condo/Coop, Rent, Parents,* or *Other*.

When discussing the Characteristic *Age*, management usually insists that it does business only with adults and, therefore, the Attributes of *Age* should start at 18 or possibly 21 and go up from there. Almost always it will be found that there are a few cases of accepted applicants who were under 18.

While deciding what Attributes are to be permissible for any Characteristic it is important to keep in mind that people who fill out documents do not always follow the instructions. Furthermore, there are some items that applicants fail to fill in at all. On applications that are submitted by mail, it is very common for applicants to leave the amount of their income blank. In other cases of blanks it is not clear if the answer to question was No or if the applicant declined to answer. Consideration must be given to these possibilities, so it is not unusual to include as possible Attributes such things as Answer Left Blank, Answer Entered But Unreadable, and Line Drawn Through Response Space.

Different Characteristics will call for different special Attributes. For example, some people will respond to the Characteristic *Applicant Age* with "Old Enough" or "Over 21" or to the Characteristic *Time at Address* with "Just Moved" or "New". Whether these non-standard responses are significant or not cannot be determined at this early stage so it is best to identify as many as possible and let the later analysis reveal their level of importance.

Two Characteristics whose attributes are chronically troublesome are *Occupation* and *Employer*. These are genuinely hard to code; that is, it is hard to select the appropriate Attributes to associate with each of them. There are literally hundreds of thousands of occupations, and this enormous multiplicity of Attributes must be boiled down to a number that can be handled conveniently.

The problem with *Employer* is similar. There are enormous numbers of employers and, if the Characteristic is to be useful, the number of its Attributes must be reduced to manageable proportions. Some decision must be made as to how to treat the "John Smith Company", a name that gives no indication whether it is a major airline or a corner fruit stand.

In the course of selecting suitable Attributes for each Characteristic it is important that there be enough Attributes at the start of the effort so that no significant Attribute is overlooked. At the same time it must be recognized that the Characteristics in the final scoring table will rarely have more than seven or eight Attributes, and will usually have five or fewer. It is with this end result in mind that the initial Attribute list should be made up. A possible list of initial Attributes for the Characteristic *Occupation* might be something like those shown in Figure 9.

Additional Attributes such as "Not Answered", "Illegible", and any

Figure 9

Possible Attributes for Characteristic:*Occupation*			
1	Executive	9	Retired
2	Homemaker	10	Sales
3	Laborer (Outside Worker)	11	Semi-Professional
4	Manager	12	Service Worker
5	Office Staff	13	Student
6	Police/Post Office/Guard	14	Trades
7	Professional	15	Unemployed, With Income
8	Production Worker	16	All Other

others considered suitable, will be appended to the list. Note carefully that there is no "right" order for these Attributes, the order in which they are written bears no necessary relationship to the importance of any of these Attributes as a predictor of future performance; the predictive power of the Attributes will not be determined until the actual data are examined. Also, the relative value of each of these Attributes will differ, sometimes strongly, from scoring system to scoring system.

Whenever possible, it is useful to retain the information going into the scoring development file in its original form. For example, it is better to record that an individual's age is 26 than to place that sample case into a bracket such as "Age between 20 and 29". That sort of grouping is better done later when there is enough information available to decide what groupings make sense. Similarly, actual dollar amounts should be recorded, rather than such things as "Over $5,000" or "Between $400 and $600". This is not always possible, however, since entering the written descriptions of all the occupations referred to on applications would present serious problems.

Conversion of data to machine usable form. The result of the process of identifying all of the eligible Characteristics and the Attributes associated with each makes it possible to construct a computer file containing substantially all the information in the documents of the sample of Goods, Bads, and Rejects.

Data entry is speeded considerably by assigning single letter codes to the Attributes that would call for multiple key strokes. For example, the Attributes of the Characteristic *Occupation* given above might be coded as shown in Figure 10, permitting the data entry operator to strike only one key rather than have to key a whole word like "Professional".

Figure 10

	Illustration of the Use of Single Letter Codes for Ease of Data Entry				
1	Executive	A	9	Retired	I
2	Homemaker	B	10	Sales	J
3	Laborer (Outside Worker)	C	11	Semi-Professional	K
4	Manager	D	12	Service Worker	L
5	Office Staff	E	13	Student	M
6	Police/Post Office/Guard	F	14	Trades	N
7	Professional	G	15	Unemployed, With Income	O
8	Production Worker	H	16	All Other	P

As a rule, numbers (such as responses to requests for *Age* or *Time At Address*) are entered as given. Some attention should be given to how dates are entered, since it may later be necessary to do arithmetic with them, such as might be needed to determine *Applicant Age* from *Date of Birth* and the date of the application.[1]

During data entry many special cases will arise that need resolution. Given the list of attributes shown in Figure 9, a data entry operator will have trouble with a retired professional who is now a student. Some rule must be constructed to cover such cases, and it must be as simple as possible, since after the scoring system is developed and installed, the people doing the scoring will use the same rule. In most situations there are very few really complex cases, and these can usually be assigned to the Attribute "All Other" without much danger. In the example given above, the decision might be that whenever a complex condition exists, use the current status; here it would assign the Attribute *Student*.

---

[1] Different countries have different customs when it comes to writing dates. Some, like the U.S., use MM/DD/YY, while others, including the U.K., use DD/MM/YY. Some applications call for the date to be expressed as YY/MM/DD, since this is the most convenient form if any arithmetic is to be done.

The structure of the computer file of the sample information can be used as the basis for a program that causes the data entry computer to interact with the data entry operators to prompt them for the item that should be entered next. It can also serve as a partial editor by refusing to accept data that is in some way incorrect. For example, the computer may reject an entry for Age that is not numeric, or an entry for Occupation that is not one of a small set of alphabetic characters such as those in the illustration given above.

Converted and Generated Characteristics. In the course of the preparation of the data for analysis, it is frequently convenient to create some new Characteristics from the information that has been entered. There are two basic types of created Characteristics. The first covers those that require some form of conversion in order to be useful. For example, some applications ask the date when the applicant took up his present residence, which must be converted to *Time at Current Address* by manipulating the given date with the date on which the application was submitted. As mentioned above, *Applicant Age* must frequently be derived from the Date of Birth shown on the application and the date of the application.

Another common case requiring conversion arises with *Income*. All income figures must be standardized if they are to be useful; that is, they must all be, say, Net Monthly Income, or perhaps Gross Weekly Income. Applications usually ask whether the income shown is Net or Gross and the time period to which the income applies. If an application in use does not ask the applicant to specify if the income is Gross or Net or ask if the income is weekly, monthly, or at some other interval, it is worth considering changing the application. However, if the applications in the sample do not carry a specification with them, some thinking must be done to decide how income is to be handled.

The second type of created Characteristic is called Generated since in this case two or more other Characteristics are used to generate an entirely new Characteristic that becomes an additional candidate for inclusion in the final scoring table, along with each of its components. In many scoring systems it is found that *Time At Last Two Addresses* is a more effective component of a scoring system than either *Time at Address* or *Time at Previous Address*.

Income, discussed above as a Characteristic requiring conversion, may also be a component of a Generated Characteristic. It is common to generate the Characteristic *Total Family Income* and include that, along with each of its components (*Income, Spouse's Income, Other Income,* etc.), as a candidate for membership in the final scoring system.

The Characteristics on the credit bureau report are frequently used to identify the most negative item or items on the report, creating a Generated Characteristic called Worst Reference.

II.2.7 Initial Enumeration.

After entering into the scoring development file all the data from the sample applications and their associated credit bureau reports, the next step is to display this information to see what it contains. The display that is produced, called Initial Enumeration, shows the actual counts of each of the attributes of each of the characteristics. The data can be displayed in many ways; Figure 11 shows one possible display that might be produced for the Characteristic *Type of Residence*.[1]

Figure 11

Hypothetical Example of Initial Enumeration for Characteristic:*Type of Residence*		
Attribute	Number of Goods	Number of Bads
Unknown	6	7
Rents Unfurnished	251	372
Rents Furnished	52	71
Buying Condo	8	8
Owns Condo	5	3
Buying House	614	507
Owns House	64	32

Note that this set of attributes is based on one particular sample. Other samples might call for a very different set. It is also a very short example of an Initial Enumeration. Two more extensive cases are shown in Figures 12 and 13. These display the initial counts of the

---

[1] It will be recalled that for the initial enumeration we use as many attributes per characteristic as we can. That is, we divide the sample as *finely* as possible. At Fair, Isaac and Co., Inc. this output is called *Fine Classing*.

Characteristics *Occupation* and *Time at Present Address.*

Figure 12

	Sample of Initial Enumeration for the Characteristic: *Occupation*				
Attribute	Number of Goods	Number of Bads	Attribute	Number of Goods	Number of Bads
Unknown	7	5	Crafts	167	200
Student	8	9	Machine Operators	88	99
Retired	33	22	Service	87	95
Professional	210	155	Laborer	35	53
Manager	133	167	Military	15	27
Clerical	110	119	Self Employed	6	5
Sales	115	54	All Other	42	69

The first use of these counts is to check for obvious coding errors. If, for example, it is found on inspection that all the applicants are 27 years old, it is obvious that an error has crept in somewhere along the line. This error could have come up in the data entry program or in some step in the data acquisition process. Wherever it came from, now is the time to correct it. While errors of this sort are rare, they can still happen even in very experienced organizations, and the time it takes to check through the documents is well spent.

The next use of the tables is to look for counts that "don't make sense". Here the liaison team has a major role, since they know their customers best and can express an opinion on suspicious looking counts. For example, while the liaison team may not know with any precision what fractions of their customers are home owners and renters, they can certainly detect a strong imbalance between the actual counts and their experience or their expectation. When an unexpected number is encountered, a search of the original data must be made to settle the issue.

One way to prepare to search through the data is to establish an audit trail, starting at the time the sample is collected. This is done by attaching a serial number to each application as soon as it becomes a member of the sample. This number is carried throughout the process. If a discrepancy is detected, a computer program can be executed to locate each of the home owners and each of the renters (to continue

Figure 13

Sample of Initial Enumaration for Characteristic: *Time at Present Address*		
Attribute	Number of Goods	Number of Bads
Unknown	59	64
New at Address	29	36
Less than 6 Months	128	194
6 Months to 1 Year	79	108
1 Yr. 1 Mo. to 1 Yr. 6 Mos.	68	87
1 Yr. 7 Mos. to 2 Yrs.	46	65
2 Yrs. 1 Mo. to 2 Yrs. 6 Mos.	37	47
2 Yrs. 7 Mos. to 3 Yrs. 6 Mos.	75	90
3 Yrs. 7 Mos. to 4 Yrs. 6 Mos.	51	64
4 Yrs. 7 Mos. to 5 Yrs. 6 Mos.	56	63
5 Yrs. 7 Mos. to 6 Yrs. 6 Mos.	44	51
6 Yrs. 7 Mos. to 7 Yrs. 6 Mos.	41	33
7 Yrs. 7 Mos. to 8 Yrs. 6 Mos.	37	25
8 Yrs. 7 Mos. to 9 Yrs. 6 Mos.	30	16
9 Yrs. 7 Mos. to 10 Yrs. 6 Mos.	35	25
10 Yrs. 7 Mos. to 12 Yrs. 6 Mos.	39	27
12 Yrs. 7 Mos. to 15 Yrs. 6 Mos.	45	37
15 Yrs. 7 Mos. to 20 Yrs. 6 Mos.	41	23
20 Yrs. 7 Mos. to 25 Yrs. 6 Mos.	30	12
25 Yrs. 7 Mos. to 30 Yrs. 6 Mos.	15	9
30 Yrs. 7 Mos. to 44 Yrs. 11 Mos.	9	4
45 Years and Over	3	1

the example) and list their sample serial numbers. A manual examination is then made of the original documents to re-tally (if necessary, by hand) the actual numbers.

The result may show that the numbers in the enumeration are correct. At this point the liaison team must decide what to do next. If the discrepancy between the counted applications and the expectation of the liaison team is sufficiently great, another sample may be extracted from the file and a special manual count made of just the item in question for comparison. This should settle the matter one way or the other. If the expectation of the liaison team turns out to have been ill founded and the counted numbers are a correct representation of the population, then the process can go forward.

If, on the other hand, the new sample produces results very different from the original, then other characteristics should be examined to see if they, too, are far from expectation. If that turns out to be the case, it may be necessary to acquire a completely new sample. Even that process would have its troubles, unless someone can come up with an explanation for the failure of the original sample to represent the underlying population.

As it happens, I have no experience with a sample that shows strange counts. The samples with which I am familiar are sufficiently large and carefully selected that the danger of misrepresenting the population is extremely small. However, it still makes sense to examine the Initial Enumeration with care to make sure that no numbers show up that are either obviously wrong or strongly counter-intuitive.

II.2.8 Classing.

The tables produced in the Initial Enumeration reveal two problems that need resolution before any meaningful analysis can be undertaken. The first problem is that, by intention, the Initial Enumeration used many more Attributes than can be used effectively to construct a robust scoring system. In the case of a scoring system that is to be used by hand (that is, not embedded in a computer of any sort) then the use of more than five or six attributes can lead to more scoring errors that the expanded attribute list can justify.

The second problem is that in many Characteristics some Attributes will show very small counts, counts that are too small to permit useful conclusions to be drawn. For example, Figure 12 shows that only 6

Goods and 5 Bads are *Self Employed.*

The solution to these two problems is called *Classing*: various Initial Enumeration Attributes are grouped together into a Classed Attribute that has a statistically significant count.

Consider, for example, the data shown in Figure 14. This Figure shows the same data as is shown in Figure 11 for *Type of Residence*, but it has been extended with some additional information. First, the percentages of the total Good and total Bads are shown for each Attribute. In addition, the Odds to be Good are shown for each Attribute with reasonable counts. The counts for *Buying Condo*, *Owns Condo*, and *Unknown* are too small to be used to calculate odds[1].

Figure 14

Attribute	Number of Goods	Number of Bads	Percent Goods	Percent Bads	Odds to be Good
Initial Enumeration of Characteristic *Type of Residence*, with Percentages and Odds to be Good					
Unknown	6	7	0.5	0.5	---
Rents Unfurnished	251	372	25.1	37.3	.67/1
Rents Furnished	52	71	5.5	6.9	.80/1
Buying Condo	8	8	0.6	1.0	---
Owns Condo	5	3	0.6	0.2	---
Buying House	614	507	61.6	50.8	1.2/1
Owns House	64	32	6.3	3.4	1.9/1

A reasonable procedure in this sort of case is to group all of the small count cases together, along with the Unknowns, into a new Attribute: *All Other*. If this is done, the remaining data look like Figure 15. This would be an acceptable classing, but an equally acceptable alternative would be to group the two Rent Attributes into one, since their Odds to be Good are quite close. If one *Rent* Attribute is produced, the data would look like Figure 16.

The case illustrated for *Type of Residence* is relatively simple; others are less so. The number of cases shown in Figure 12 for *Unknown*,

---

[1]The Odds are calculated by dividing the Percent Goods by the Percent Bads. Other measures can be used to indicate the importance of a particular attribute. A commonly used measure is Weight of Evidence, a more complex statistic than the calculation of Odds, but Odds will better serve the purpose of this book.

Figure 15

Classed Data for *Type of Residence*					
Attribute	Number of Goods	Number of Bads	Percent Goods	Percent Bads	Odds to be Good
Rents Unfurnished	251	372	25.1	37.2	.67/1
Rents Furnished	52	71	5.5	6.9	.80/1
House	678	539	67.8	53.9	1.26/1
All Other	19	18	1.9	1.8	1.1/1

Figure 16

Alternative Classed Data for *Type of Residence*					
Attribute	Number of Goods	Number of Bads	Percent Goods	Percent Bads	Odds to be Good
Rent	303	443	30.3	44.3	.68/1
House	678	539	67.8	53.9	1.26/1
All Other	19	18	1.9	1.8	1.1/1

Students, *Retired*, *Self-Employed*, *Laborers*, *Military* and *All Other* are insufficient for further analysis on their own. The safest course is to group them all together into the Attribute, *All other*, as is shown in Figure 17.

Figure 17

Partial Classing of *Occupation*					
Attribute	Number of Goods	Number of Bads	Percent Goods	Percent Bads	Odds to be Good
Professional	210	155	19.9	14.4	1.38/1
Manager	133	167	12.7	15.5	.82/1
Clerical	110	119	10.5	11.0	.95/1
Sales	115	54	11.0	5.0	2.2/1
Crafts	167	200	16.0	18.5	.86/1
Machine Operator	88	99	8.4	9.2	.91/1
Service	87	95	8.4	8.8	.95/1
All Other	146	190	13.9	17.6	.79/1

Further examination shows that the Attributes *Clerical, Machine Operators,* and *Service* all have Odds to be Good that are very nearly equal. Grouping these three Attributes together gives much higher counts for the Goods and Bads of the new Attribute. Similarly, the Attribute *Manager* has Odds to be Good very close to those of the new *All Other* Attribute, suggesting that these two can be grouped together. When these two groupings suggested above are carried out, the classed data for the Characteristic *Occupation* looks like Figure 18. Keep in mind that this example has been constructed to demonstrate a process and does not constitute a set of instructions for how *Occupation* should be classed. ★

Figure 18

Classed Data for *Occupation*					
Attribute	Number of Goods	Number of Bads	Percent Goods	Percent Bads	Odds to be Good
Professional	210	155	19.9	14.4	1.38/1
Machine Operator, Clerical, Service	285	313	26.9	29.0	.92/1
Sales	115	54	10.9	5.0	2.2/1
Crafts	167	200	15.8	18.5	.85/1
All Other	279	357	26.6	33.1	.80/1

There is an extremely important role in the Classing process for the Liaison team. However statistically valid a scoring table may be, its effectiveness will depend, in part, on the attitude of the user staff who will actually be doing the scoring when the score table is in operation. If the user's staff finds some of the classed groupings unpalatable, the effectiveness of the operation of the scoring system may be seriously impaired.[1]

In the example in Figure 18 the *Managers* have been grouped with *All Other*. While this is fully justified by the data in the illustration, the user or some of the user's staff might feel that this grouping is unacceptable. In such a case it makes operational sense to keep the two Attributes separate, since there are sufficient counts in the Goods and the Bads of each. If this Characteristic appears in the final scoring

---

[1] If scoring is embedded inside a computer, as is the case in many installations, this problem is not so severe since only a much smaller group needs to be convinced of the validity of the scoring table. The individuals entering the application data into the computer do not know what is in the scoring table.

table, it is not unlikely that the two Attributes will have the same score, but experience in such cases suggests that the user's staff will be satisfied as long as the two are separate.

Characteristics such as *Time at Address*, *Years on Job*, *Income*, and *Age* have Attributes that start at zero and go up steadily to some high number. Such Characteristics are referred to as *Continuous*. Characteristics such as *Occupation* or *Bank Reference* are called *Discrete* Characteristics since their Attributes do not fall into any particular order. Discrete Characteristics can be classed by their count and their Odds to be Good.

However, in the case of a Continuous Characteristic, grouping the first, seventh, and ninth Attributes, even though their Odds to be Good might be close, would make it difficult to manage the scoring table and would appear to violate "common sense". It is better to group adjacent Attributes, even at the cost of a small amount of predictive power in the final result. This situation is illustrated in Figures 19 and 20.

The number of Classed Attributes that should be created in any particular case depends on the actual counts that are available in the Initial Enumeration Attributes, on the opinions of the user, and on whether the score table is to be used as part of a computer application of scoring or by hand. An Attribute can stand on its own if it has a count in both the Goods and the Bads of 100 or more. However, this might lead to a number of Classed Attributes greater than five or six and, therefore, somewhat unwieldy for manual use. On the other hand, if the scoring table is to be applied inside a computer program, the more Attributes, the better.

Treatment of Blanks.

When an applicant does not answer a question on a credit application, either accidentally or intentionally, he creates a special problem for the developers of a scoring system. This happens frequently, especially on applications that are submitted by mail.

Blanks can be handled in two ways; they can be viewed as containing predictive information or as containing none.

If blanks are viewed as having no predictive information, then all the blank cases should be kept separate from other data that might contain

Figure 19

Attribute	Number of Goods	Number of Bads	Percent Goods	Percent Bads	Odds to be Good	Classed Attribute
Sample Enumeration of Characteristic *Time at Present Address* With Percents and Odds to be Good						
Unknown	59	64	5.9	6.4	.92/1	
New at Address	29	36	2.9	3.3	.88/1	#1
Less than 6 Months	128	194	12.8	17.9	.72/1	#1
6 Months to 1 Year	79	108	7.9	10.0	.79/1	#1
1 Yr. 1 Mo. to 1 Yr. 6 Mos.	68	87	6.8	8.0	.85/1	#1
1 Yr. 7 Mos. to 2 Yrs.	46	65	4.6	6.0	.77/1	#1
2 Yrs. 1 Mo. to 2 Yrs. 6 Mos.	37	47	3.7	4.3	.86/1	#1
2 Yrs. 7 Mos. to 3 Yrs. 6 Mos.	75	90	7.5	8.3	.90/1	#2
3 Yrs. 7 Mos. to 4 Yrs. 6 Mos.	51	64	5.1	5.9	.86/1	#2
4 Yrs. 7 Mos. to 5 Yrs. 6 Mos.	56	63	5.6	5.8	.96/1	#2
5 Yrs. 7 Mos. to 6 Yrs. 6 Mos.	44	51	4.4	4.7	.93/1	#2
6 Yrs. 7 Mos. to 7 Yrs. 6 Mos.	41	33	4.1	3.1	1.3/1	#3
7 Yrs. 7 Mos. to 8 Yrs. 6 Mos.	37	25	3.7	2.3	1.4/1	#3
8 Yrs. 7 Mos. to 9 Yrs. 6 Mos.	30	16	3.0	1.5	2/1	#3
9 Yrs. 7 Mos. to 10 Yrs. 6 Mos.	35	25	3.5	2.3	1.5/1	#3
10 Yrs. 7 Mos. to 12 Yrs. 6 Mos.	39	27	3.9	2.5	1.6/1	#3
12 Yrs. 7 Mos. to 15 Yrs. 6 Mos.	45	37	4.5	3.4	1.3/1	#3
15 Yrs. 7 Mos. to 20 Yrs. 6 Mos.	41	23	4.1	2.1	1.9/1	#3
20 Yrs. 7 Mos. to 25 Yrs. 6 Mos.	30	12	3.0	1.1	2.7/1	#3
25 Yrs. 7 Mos. to 30 Yrs. 6 Mos.	15	9	1.5	0.8	1.9/1	#3
30 Yrs. 7 Mos. to 44 Yrs. 11 Mos.	9	4	0.9	0.4	2.3/1	#3
45 Years and Over	3	1	0.3	0.1	3/1	#3

Figure 20

Classed Data for Characteristic:*Time at Present Address*					
Attribute	Number of Goods	Number of Bads	Percent Goods	Percent Bads	Odds to be Good
Unknown	59	64	5.9	6.4	.92/1
New to 2 Years	350	490	35.1	45.3	.77/1
2 Yrs. 1 Mo. to 6 Yrs. 6 Mos.	263	315	26.3	29.1	.90/1
6 Yrs. 7 Mos. and Up	325	212	32.6	19.6	1.66/1

predictive information. From that point on, throughout the process of computing the scoring table, the Attribute *Blank* is forced to show no predictive power. This means that for a question that is left blank by an applicant, the user of the scoring table draws no conclusion whatever from the Characteristic. In effect, for that Applicant, that Characteristic is treated as if it is not part of the scoring table.

There are cases, however, where a user may elect to draw a conclusion from a blank. For example, in the case of a mail-in application for a credit card a user may decide to examine the blank Attribute in each Characteristic to see if it contains information. If it is found that 80% of the Good applicants but only 10% of the Bad applicants leave some particular attribute blank, the user may decide to consider Blank to be a valid Attribute of the Characteristic and allow it into the scoring table.

II.2.9 The Calculation of Score Points.

When the Attributes of each Characteristic have been classed, the next step is the preparation of the score table. This is a table that shows, for each Attribute, the number of points that are to be awarded to an applicant showing that Attribute. Examples of score tables are shown in Figure 1, in the Introduction, and in Figures 29, 30, and 31, below. The sum of the points awarded from the appropriate Attribute of each Characteristic is the *credit score*, usually referred to simply as the *score*.

Since this is not a treatise on multivariate statistics, I will not attempt to expound on the various ways in which score points can be calculated from the classed data. Various procedures are available for this calculation, and all of them are reasonably effective. Whatever method is used, it will be found that when a body of Good and Bad accounts are scored using the points shown in the score table, both the Goods and the Bads have some members with low scores and some members with high scores. However, if the scoring system has predictive power, more Good accounts will have high scores and more Bad accounts will have low scores.[1]

Figure 21 shows what happens when we plot a graph of the fraction of accounts that fall in each score interval.

Figure 21

Percentages of Good and Bad Accounts by Score Interval

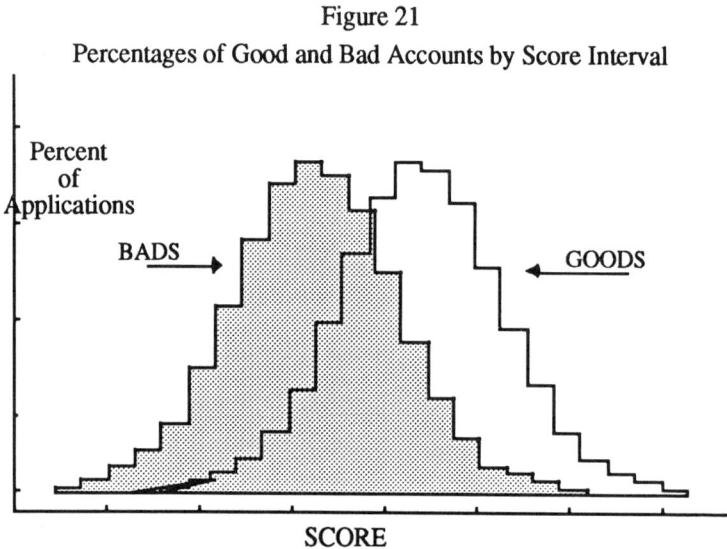

Figure 22 shows the same information, but with the curves smoothed. Both the Good and the Bad accounts are seen to be distributed about average scores. In this example, the Good accounts are clustered around 218 while the Bad accounts are clustered around 205. The figure also shows that there are Bad accounts with high scores and Good accounts with low scores. This is a numerical reflection of the experience of every credit officer; a few accounts that appeared at application time to be excellent risks turn out badly while some applications that appeared quite risky turn out to perform in exemplary fashion.

Figure 23 shows the effect of setting a minimum acceptable score. A line has been shown at a score of 200 points. If only applications

[1] It has become the custom in much of the credit scoring field to construct score tables so that high scores indicate low risk (high Odds to be Good) while low scores indicate high risk. This is an entirely arbitrary choice.

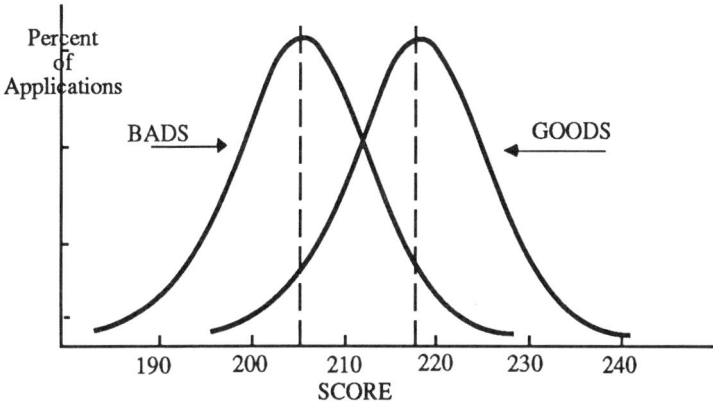

Figure 22

Percentages of Good and Bad Accounts - Smoothed Data

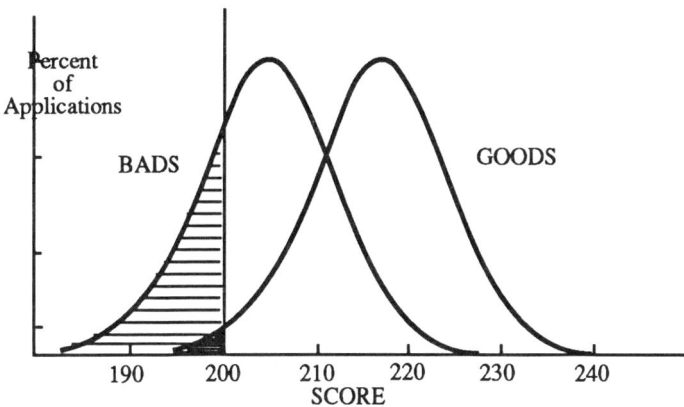

Figure 23

Illustration of the Effect of a Cut-Off Score

scoring that value or higher were accepted, the enterprise using the scoring system would find that it is avoiding the body of Bads to the left of the line, shown lined, but would forego that smaller body of Good accounts to the left of the line, shown dark. Moving the minimum score line to the right will cut off an even higher fraction of the Bad accounts but will forego a larger fraction of Good accounts, while moving the minimum score line to the left will accomplish the opposite. The score at which the minimum score line is set is called the *cut-off score* and will be discussed in more detail in Section II.3.2.

Since both the curves actually tail off indefinitely in both directions, there is no score at which it can be guaranteed that no Bads will be taken.

These curves do not represent the actual numbers of Good and Bad accounts, only their percentages. In practice there are far fewer Bads than Goods and a graph of the actual counts of Good and Bad cases looks more line the curves shown in Figure 24.

Figure 24

Smoothed Distributions of Numbers of Accounts

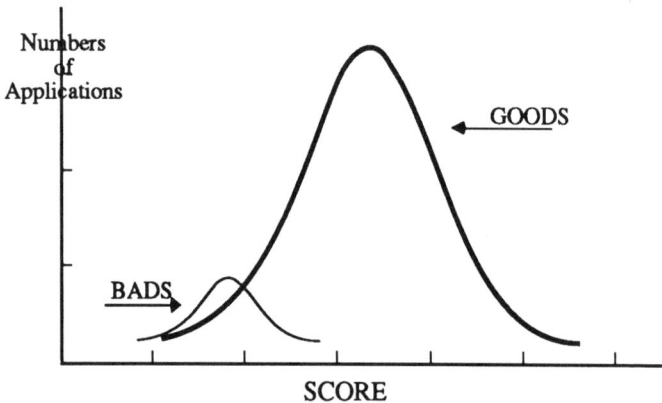

The relative power of two scoring systems to predict risk is demonstrated by Figure 25. Both pairs of curves show the smoothed distributions of the fractions of Good and Bad accounts by score. If a cut-off score is selected at any point along the horizontal axis and a minimum score line is erected there, as is shown in the Figure, the upper pair of curves show that about half of the Bad accounts would be accepted. In the case of the lower pair of curves only about one quarter of the Bads would be accepted, while the same number of Goods are taken in the two cases. The scoring table that produced the lower set of curves is, therefore, the more powerful and the more effective in separating Good accounts from Bad.

This ability to measure the performance of a scoring table is one of the more important features of credit scoring. Two scoring systems can be compared by using both to score a single body of Good and Bad accounts and then measuring the distance between the mean scores in the two cases. The one with the larger separation is better than the other.

Figure 25

Comparison of the Power of Two Scoring Systems

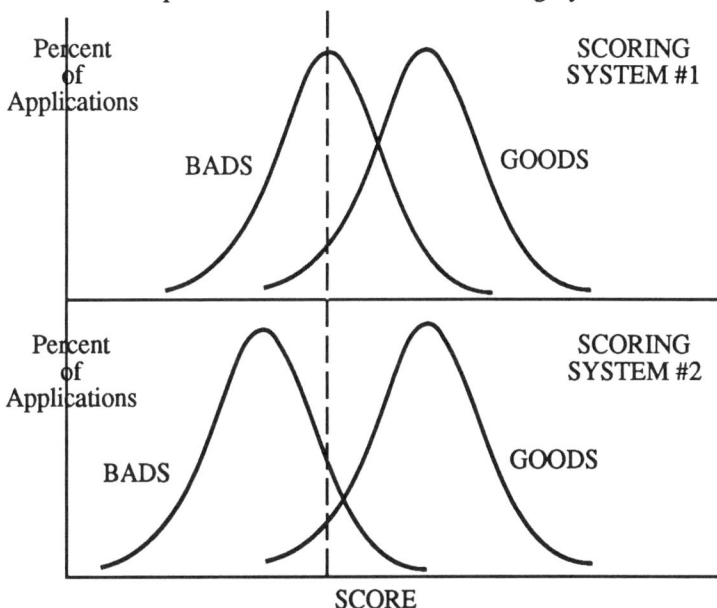

Augmentation — The Reject Inference.

So far I have discussed only the Good and the Bad accounts and have paid little attention to the applications that were rejected. The flow of applications is shown in Figure 26. Of the applications received, some fraction will be declined while the accepted applications will finally divide into Good and Bad accounts. This fraction can vary, depending on the enterprise and the policy it is following at the time, from a very low figure (5 to 10%) to a very high figure (60 to 75%).

If a scoring table is developed using only the information on known Good and known Bad accounts, it misrepresents the actual population through the door, since it ignores the information available about the rejected applicants. Just as there are Bad accounts among those that are accepted, it is reasonable to expect that there could have been some Good accounts among those that were rejected.

Since the goal is to discontinue the current evaluation procedure and apply the scoring system to the population through the door, not just to those that would be accepted using the traditional method, it is necessary to base it on the information that comes through the door,

Figure 26

Normal Flow of Applications

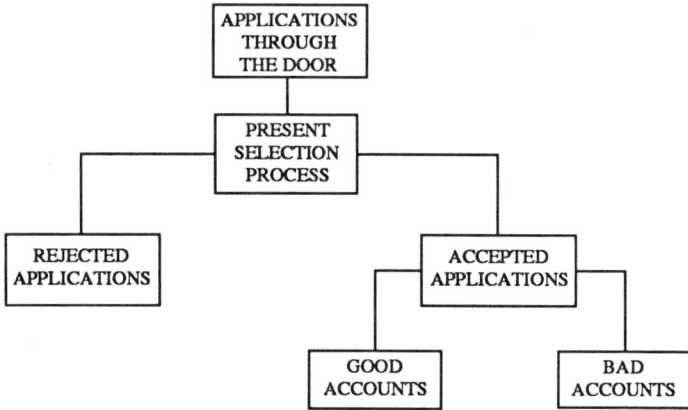

not only on information from the accepted applications.

What must be done is to infer, in some manner, how the rejected applicants would have performed had they been accepted. Clearly, we cannot *know* how they would have performed, since they did not have the chance to do so, but it is possible, on the information that is supplied on the applications, to make an inference. If we can infer what fraction of the rejects would have been Good and what fraction would have been Bad we can add the Known Goods and the Inferred Goods to get a figure for the Total Goods, and add the Known Bads and the Inferred Bads to get a total for the Total Bads through the door.

This process is illustrated in Figure 27. The body of applicants is divided between Accepts and Rejects. The Acceptees are divided, in their turn, between Known Good and Known Bad, since we have performance information on these. The Rejects are to be divided into Inferred Goods and Inferred Bads, so that it is possible to form the two numbers for Total Goods and Total Bads through the door.

The generic name for the process of making an inference regarding the rejected Applications is Augmentation. The derivation comes from the idea that the number of Known Goods is augmented by the number of Inferred Goods to find the total number of Goods in the basic population.

Figure 27

Determination of Behavior of Population Through the Door
Through Reject nference

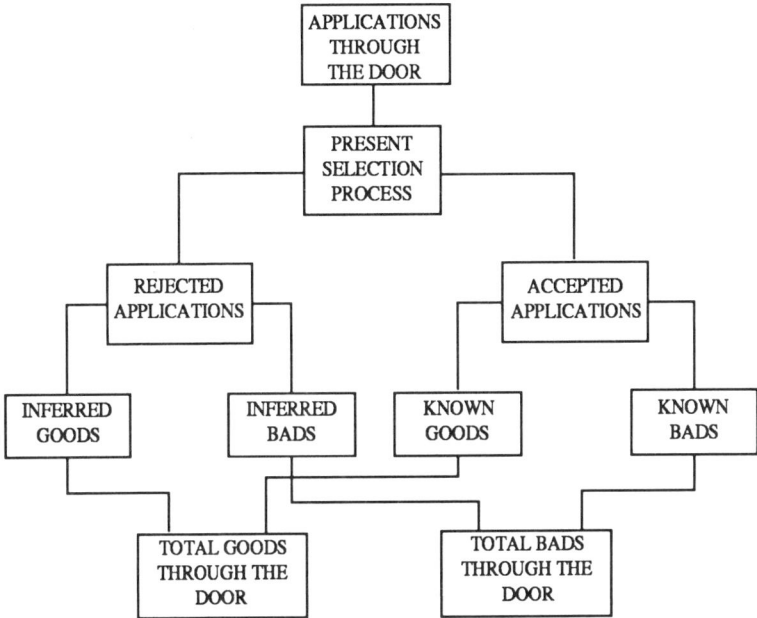

A variety of Augmentation procedures are available, every one being subject to some sort of criticism. The method least subject to criticism, but by far the most costly, is to accept everyone who applies for some period, until a sufficiently large group has been assembled, say 10,000 cases. When these cases are examined after their performance becomes known, it is possible to get a feeling for the underlying number of Goods and Bads in the total population.

Naturally, this would be an expensive process, since accounts that would have been rejected by the traditional methods would be accepted and the enterprise would pay the price for the additional bad accounts. Furthermore, accepting a body of accounts at one time does not necessarily mean that the proportion of Good and Bad accounts will remain the same over time. Nevertheless, it is, as I said, the procedure least open to criticism.

The process of Augmentation provides one piece of very important information; the Population Odds. (See Section II.1.2) If all applicants are accepted (either in reality or by inference) then the ratio of the total number of Goods to the total number of Bads is the Population Odds; how many Goods there are for each Bad in the whole applicant population. The Population Odds in most cases falls between 8 to 1 and 20 to 1, although very sharp departures in both directions have been observed.

Every enterprise draws its customers from a particular population, so that it understandable that the Population Odds will be different for different businesses. While the Population Odds are not always dramatically different from one enterprise to another, its determination is not only of general interest but is necessary in order to calculate the total odds represented by any score. The manner in which the Population Odds are determined is illustrated in Figure 28, using a hypothetical group of 10,000 applications and a representative Bad rate and reject percentage.

Figure 28
Calculation of Population Odds

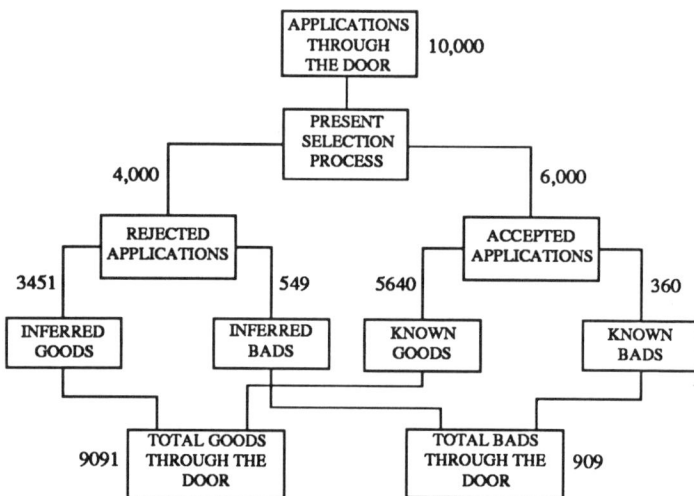

9091 Goods and 909 Bads corresponds to 9091/909 or Odds of
10 to 1 to be Good

Score Point Restrictions.

Other things being equal, the computation of score points should proceed directly from the classed data, whatever it may be, without the injection of opinion, prejudice, or other modification. However, when this procedure is followed, the results may violate some law or regulation, or they may be felt by the user to offend "common sense".

In the United States there is legislation and regulation on the Federal level that affects consumer credit in general and credit scoring in particular. In addition to other requirements, the Act states that it shall not be considered discriminatory "to use any empirically derived credit system which considers age if such system is demonstrably and statistically sound in accordance with the regulations of the Board, except that in the operation of such system the age of an elderly applicant may not be assigned a negative factor or value". [1]

In the cases where the Characteristic *Age* is a candidate for inclusion in the scoring table, it is possible that the data might determine that individuals over 62 should receive fewer points than applicants at some lesser age.[2] Since this is specifically forbidden by the Act and the Regulation, it is necessary to ensure that the Attribute of the Characteristic *Age* that includes the elderly receives no fewer points than the highest of all the other Attributes.

To accomplish this a process known as Restriction was developed that interferes with the score point calculation program by assigning to the Attribute that includes elderly applicants the highest score weight of all of the other Attributes of that Characteristic, unless the program would have assigned still higher points to this group had the Restriction not been applied. As it happens, it is rarely necessary to invoke this Restriction, since in almost all cases the elderly applicants are awarded high scores by the calculation process, due to their generally superior performance, but it must be available in those cases where this does not happen.

The Restriction facility is handy for other purposes as well. It can be used to modify the score points when the results appear to contradict "common sense". For example, a score table may award carpenters more points than, say, physicians, or it may show that more points are awarded for people with short job tenure than to people who have been on the job for a long time.

It is not unknown to find that points increase as income increases, except that at some intermediate income there can be a sudden dip in score. Cases like these can cause the user to have doubts about the validity of the scoring system and hesitate to use it.

---

[1] The "Board" refers to The Board of Governors of the Federal Reserve System.

[2] 62 is the age at which an applicant is considered elderly by Regulation B of the Board.

The Liaison Team is particularly valuable in the area of Restrictions, since it can provide information as to the perception of management of the Characteristics that are eligible to appear in the score table. If management has strong feelings as to the relative importance of different occupations, it may request that the score points follow some specific order. If management feels that income should progressively increase in score value, it may request that a restriction forcing this pattern be imposed.

While the Restriction operator is a convenience and can improve the acceptability of the end result, it is not without cost. The cost may be the minor one that an additional Characteristic enters the scoring table. ★ If the information denied to the score table by the restrictions cannot be found in some previously omitted Characteristic, the overall power of the resulting scoring table is diminished. Except in the case of Age where the restriction is required by law, it is advisable to produce the score table without restrictions so that it can be compared with the results with the restrictions so that Management can decide whether it wants to pay the price that the restrictions demand in terms of the reduced power of the scoring system.

Credit Bureau Information.

So far I have discussed score point calculation as if all eligible Characteristics were considered at the same time. While there is a good deal to be said for that procedure, there is also argument for an alternative. While credit bureau information is known to be extremely helpful in the determination of credit risk, it costs money and, in many cases, no report is available.

In the light of the cost of reports and their possible absence, the score point calculation program can be modified to produce a score table in two parts, the first containing points only for those Characteristics available on the application and the second containing points for predictive information from Credit Bureau Characteristics not already included in the score points from the application. When this is done an applicant can be scored on application data alone to see if a decision can be made on the basis of this information. If the score on application information is so low that no matter how good the credit bureau score may be, the final total will not exceed the cut-off, then that application can be rejected without the expense in time or money of getting a bureau report.

The Score Table.

The score point calculation program with which I am familiar computes points for each Characteristic that can be either positive or negative. Figure 29 is a fictitious example of what the initial output might look like. For every Characteristic there is an Attribute labeled "Blank", which is fixed at 0 points. In the Characteristic *Worst Credit Reference* this is the *No Record* Attribute.

Figure 29 - Example of Application Scoring System

Years on Job	Less than 6 Months -9	Six Mos. to 1 Yr 6 Mos 0	1 Yr 7 Mos to 6 Yrs 8 Mos 6	6 Yrs 9 Mos to 10 Yrs 5 Mos 13	10 Yrs 6 Mos or more 25	Blank 0	
Own or Rent	Own or Buying 15	Rent -5	All Other 2	Blank 0			
Banking	Checking Account 5	Savings Account 0	Checking and Savings 14	None -17	Blank 0		
Major Credit Card	Yes 10	No -6	Blank 0				
Occupation	Retired 21	Professional 16	Clerical 7	Sales -2	Service -8	All Other 7	Blank 0
Age of Applicant	18 to 25 -3	26 to 31 -8	32 to 34 0	35 to 51 4	52 to 61 12	62 and Over 18	Blank 0
Worst Credit Reference	Major Derogatory -15	Minor Derogatory -4	No Record -2	One Satisfactory 9	Two or More Satisfactory 18	No Investig. 0	

If this score table is to be embedded in a computer program it can be left as it is, since computers if programmed correctly will carry out the arithmetic without error. However, if the table is to be used for the manual calculation of scores there is some advantage in removing as many of the negative signs as possible, since people occasionally err in mixing addition and subtraction. Figure 30 shows the result of adding enough points to all of the Attributes of each Characteristic so that all weights are positive or zero. A total of 53 points have been added to the scores in Figure 29, enough points being added to each

Figure 30 - Example of Application Scoring Table, All Scores positive or Zero

Years on Job	Less than 6 Months	Six Mos. to 1 Yr 6 Mos	1 Yr 7 Mos to 6 Yrs 8 Mos	6 Yrs 9 Mos to 10 Yrs 5 Mos	10 Yrs 6 Mos or more	Blank	
	0	9	15	22	34	9	
Own or Rent	Own or Buying	Rent	All Other	Blank			
	20	0	7	5			
Banking	Checking Account	Savings Account	Checking and Savings	None	Blank		
	22	17	31	0	17		
Major Credit Card	Yes	No	Blank				
	16	0	6				
Occupation	Retired	Professional	Clerical	Sales	Service	All Other	Blank
	29	24	15	6	0	15	8
Age of Applicant	18 to 25	26 to 31	32 to 34	35 to 51	52 to 61	62 and Over	Blank
	5	0	8	12	20	26	8
Worst Credit Reference	Major Derogatory	Minor Derogatory	No Record	One Satisfactory	Two or More Satisfactory	No Invest.	
	-15	-4	-2	9	18	0	

Characteristic (except *Worst Credit Reference*) to raise the largest negative score to zero. When the scores are made positive, the Attribute for Blank into which blanks and other apparent errors have been put, is no longer zero.

The scores for the Attributes of the credit bureau Characteristic (*Worst Reference*) have retained their negatives. Some users may prefer to have all of the numbers positive, including those associated with credit bureau information, but it has been my experience that many users prefer a negative score for derogatory information.

In addition to making all or most of the scores positive, some users like to have the cut-off score set at a round number like 200. If the cut-off score, set to accept, say, 60% of the applicants, as will be discussed in Section II.3.2, turns out to be 159 when calculated from the score points in Figure 30, distributing 41 points throughout the table will shift the cut-off to 200. Figure 31 shows the results of this process. Six points have been added to each of the Attributes of the Characteristic *Major Credit Card* while 7 points have been added to

Figure 31 - Example of Application Scoring Table, All Scores
Positrive or Zero, Including Additive Points

Years on Job	Less than 6 Months 7	Six Mos. to 1 Yr 6 Mos 16	1 Yr 7 Mos to 6 Yrs 8 Mos 22	6 Yrs 9 Mos to 10 Yrs 5 Mos 29	10 Yrs 6 Mos or more 41	Blank 16	
Own or Rent	Own or Buying 27	Rent 7	All Other 14	Blank 12			
Banking	Checking Account 29	Savings Account 24	Checking and Savings 38	None 7	Blank 24		
Major Credit Card	Yes 22	No 6	Blank 12				
Occupation	Retired 36	Professional 31	Clerical 22	Sales 13	Service 7	All Other 22	Blank 15
Age of Applicant	18 to 25 12	26 to 31 7	32 to 34 15	35 to 51 19	52 to 61 27	62 and Over 33	Blank 15
Worst Credit Reference	Major Derogatory -15	Minor Derogatory -4	No Record -2	One Satisfactory 9	Two or More Satisfactory 18	No Invest. 0	

the Attributes of all of the other Characteristics except *Worst Reference*.

The addition of points to all of the Attributes of some or all of the Characteristics changes the score that any applicant will receive, but it does not change the rank order of any group of scored applicants, since they will all receive the same number of additive points.

II.2.10 Statistics and Strategy.

While the score table is the most visible component of a scoring system, it is not the only one. The other major component is the set of statistical outputs which management uses to decide how the scoring system is to be operated.

The statistical tables are produced by scoring the entire body of the sample data with the newly developed scores, and tallying the results.

The first table, a small part of which is shown in part in Figure 32, shows how many Goods and how many Bads were awarded each possible score, from low to high, and also shows the Odds to be Good at each score. For example, if management decides that the lowest acceptable score is to be 200 points, this table shows that the enterprise has elected to accept applicants with odds to be Good of 16 to 1 or higher.[1]

Figure 32
Portion of Table of Interval Statistics

SCORE	GOODS	BADS	ODDS
190	60	10	10.7
191	66	13	11.2
192	117	22	11.7
193	106	20	12.3
194	69	14	12.8
195	58	10	13.4
196	152	17	13.8
197	96	15	14.3
198	135	19	14.9
199	101	14	15.4
200	140	8	16.0
201	144	15	16.6
202	177	15	17.2
203	159	20	17.7
204	176	14	18.3
205	182	16	18.8

The figures in this table are illustrative, and they have been rounded to make the presentation more easily understandable. Only a small part of the table that is actually produced is shown here. In a real case the table that is delivered to a user is four or five pages long and covers the whole range of approximately 250 scores.

The second table, Figure 33, shows the same information (along with some total data) but now in ascending cumulative form. That is, at each score it shows the total count of all the scores lower than and including that score. For example, Figure 33 shows that 3381 of the

[1]The Odds to be Good cannot be calculated from this table but are produced by the manufacturer from the smoothed curves fitted to the distributions of Good and Bad accounts, and is beyond the scope of this book.

Goods have scores of 199 or below, while 622 of the Bads have scores in that range.

Figure 33
Portion of Table of
Ascending Cumulative Statistics

SCORE	CUM. GOODS	CUM. BADS	CUM. G + B	% OF TOTAL
190	2481	478	2959	29.6
191	2547	491	3038	30.4
192	2664	513	3177	31.8
193	2770	533	3303	33.0
194	2839	547	3386	33.9
195	2897	557	3454	34.5
196	3049	574	3623	36.2
197	3145	589	3734	37.3
198	3280	608	3888	38.9
199	3381	622	4003	40.0
200	3521	630	4151	41.5
201	3665	645	4310	43.1
202	3842	660	4502	45.0
203	4001	680	4681	46.8
204	4177	694	4871	48.7
205	4359	710	5069	50.7

The third table is the reverse of the second, showing the information in descending cumulative form, as illustrated in Figure 34. This figure shows that 5710 of the Goods have scores of 200 or over, while only 287 of the Bads are in this range. If the cut-off score is set at 200 the enterprise will accept 60% of the applicants.

These tables provide the user management with the information it needs to decide on a strategy for the use of the scoring system. Management starts from a knowledge of the current state of the credit portfolio. Consider, for example, an enterprise that accepts 60% of the applicants and where 6% of those accepted turn out to be Bad, following the flow of applications shown in Figure 28.

The question is: What will happen if 60% acceptance is continued when the score table is in use. Figure 34 shows that if the cut-off score is set at 200 points, a total of 5,997 of an applicant population of 10,000, or 60% of the applicants, will have that score or higher. It

Figure 34

Portion of Table of
Descending Cumulative Statistics

SCORE	CUM. GOODS	CUM. BADS	CUM. G + B	% OF TOTAL
190	6670	441	7111	71.1
191	6610	431	7041	70.4
192	6544	418	6962	69.6
193	6427	396	6823	68.2
194	6321	376	6697	67.0
195	6252	362	6614	66.1
196	6194	352	6546	65.5
197	6042	335	6377	63.8
198	5946	320	6266	62.7
199	5811	301	6112	61.1
200	5710	287	5997	60.0
201	5570	279	5849	58.5
202	5426	264	5690	56.9
203	5249	249	5498	55.0
204	5090	229	5319	53.2
205	4914	213	5127	51.3

also shows that 287 of those accepted will turn out to be Bad. This is
4.8% of the accepted accounts (287 out of 5997). Since the current
bad rate is 6%, or 360 of those acceptees out of 10,000 applicants, the
use of the scoring system will avoid 360 minus 287, or 73 of the Bads.
This represents a 20.0% reduction in Bads, and all the costs associated with them, with no change in acceptance rate.

Alternatively, management might examine what would happen to the
volume of acceptees if the *number* of Bads remains the same. Figure
34 shows that there are 362 Bads at a score of 195 or higher, which is
5.4% of the total number of accepted accounts. This row also shows
that a total of 6,614 out of 10,000 applicants would be accepted if the
cut-off score is 195, an increase in volume of over 10%. This increase
in volume is all profit, since the number of Bads has not changed and
all the increased acceptees are Good. These two alternatives are
summarized in Figure 35.

The two alternatives shown in Figure 35 are, of course, in no way

Figure 35
Examples of Alternative Strategies

Case 1 No Change in Volume (Acceptance Rate 60%)	Case 2 No Change in Number of Bads (Bad Rate 6%)
Cut-off Score 200 Points	Cut-off Score 195 Points
Total Number of Goods Accepted -- 5710 Total Number of Bads Accepted -- 287 Total Acceptees -- 5997	Total Number of Goods Accepted -- 6252 Total Number of Bads Accepted -- 362 Total Acceptees -- 6614
Current Bads -- 360 Bads Accepted With Score -- 287 Reduction in Bads -- 73 Percentage Reduction in Bads -- 20.2%	Total Accepted With Score -- 6614 Current Total Accepted -- 6000 Increase in Acceptees -- 614 Percentage Increase in Volume -- 10.2%

limiting. Management may decide on any acceptance rate it finds desirable, and when it does so, can look at the table and estimate what the result can be expected to be. If the acceptance rate is raised, the number of Bads will go up, along with the total volume of business. If the acceptance rate is reduced, the number of Bads will go down, but so will the revenue since there will be fewer Goods doing business with the enterprise. The range of choice is large, as is shown by the graph in Figure 36. ★

This graph is produced from the information in the Descending Cumulative Table, Figure 34 and the application flow information in Figure 28. A user may elect to operate anywhere along the strategy curve. He may set either the bad rate or the acceptance rate; either will fix the other.

II.2.11   The Delivered Product.

In addition to the score table and the statistical tables discussed in the two previous sections, the product delivered by the manufacturer must include scoring instructions and installation instructions.

The scoring instructions explain in detail how scoring is to be carried out and how individual items of information on an application or a credit bureau report are to be assigned to Attributes of Characteristics. The installation instructions discuss the problems involved in the installation of a scoring system, the matters which management must consider, and the decisions that management must make in the course of the installation. It also reviews the decisions that management has made during the development of the scoring system.

Figure 36
Strategy Opportunities and Current Strategy

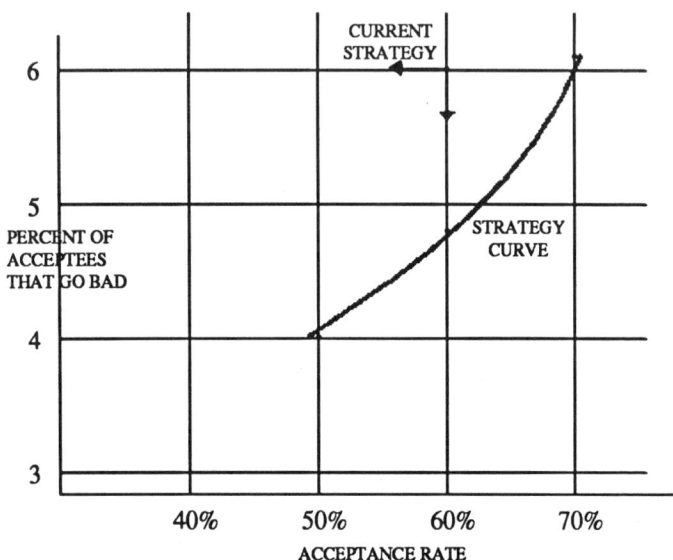

II.2.11.1 Scoring Instructions.

The Scoring Instructions tell the individuals processing incoming applications how the information on the applications is to be assigned to individual Characteristics and their Attributes. These instructions must be the same as the instructions used when the original sample data was converted to machine usable form at the time the scoring system was manufactured. For many Characteristics, such as *Age*, the instructions are almost obvious if an age is given on the application. However, it is necessary to describe clearly how a blank or an unexpected response, such as "Old enough", is to be handled. In most cases both of these (and similar) responses are assigned to the Attribute "Blank" indicating that there is no information to be inferred from the data, but special cases may exist.

One item that requires very careful explanation is the Characteristic *Occupation*. There are enormous numbers of occupations, and this huge multiplicity has been reduced to a half a dozen or so Attributes in the score table. It is important that the individuals doing the scoring assign occupations in the same way that they were assigned during the development of the scoring system, so extensive documentation is usually provided.

In the initial enumeration, the Characteristic *Occupation* may be divided into 20 or more individual Attributes. Figure 37 shows one possible set of Attributes for *Occupation*, quite different from the list shown in Figure 12. Various other lists are possible and will depend on the experience of the manufacturer and the specific nature of the business of the user.

Figure 37
Example of Possible Attributes of Characteristic *Occupation*

1	Driver
2	Executive
3	Guard
4	Homemaker
5	Laborer, Outside Worker
6	Manager
7	Military
8	Office Staff
9	Owner of a Business
10	Production Worker
11	Professional
12	Retired
13	Sales
14	Semiprofessional
15	Service
16	Student
17	Trades
18	Unemployed (with income)
19	Unemployed (without income)
20	All Other

The coding instructions specify in detail just what is included in each of these attributes, since there can be different views as to how individual occupations should be classified. For example, if occupation is given as "Personnel Officer" the scorer will have to know if it should be classified as Office Staff, Professional, Semiprofessional, Manager, or be included in some other Attribute.

The Liaison team has a part to play in developing the coding instructions, since the user's view as to how occupations should be classified will be given great weight by the manufacturer. It is in the manufacturer's interest, as well as that of the user, that scoring be done accurately, and individual scorers will be more likely to accept the scoring system and use it in accordance with the user's policy if the classification of *Occupation* is consistent with the attitudes of the user.

The types of occupations to be included in any one of the attributes in the list given in Figure 37 must be set forth in as much detail as possible, giving attention (with the help of the Liaison team) to any special occupations in their field of business. For example, if the delivered scoring system is to be used in an area heavily involved in the lumber industry, the Characteristic *Occupation* must account for the major job titles of the lumber industry, while if the area has a large automobile industry, it must include the major job titles of that business.

An example of the sort of list that is provided in the coding instructions to make clear which types of work are to be included in any one of the Attributes of *Occupation* is given in Figure 38. Note that the 46 Occupations shown in Figure 38 will be included in one Attribute: *Semiprofessional*. Other Initial Enumeration Attributes will be grouped together into other Classed Attributes, usually groupings that "common sense" would suggest. Professional and Executive or Professional and Semiprofessional, or all three, are very often grouped together in the Classed Enumeration. Similarly, Production Workers and Trades are often grouped together. Many other "reasonable" associations are made in various cases.

Figure 38

Example of Occupations Assigned to the Attribute
Semiprofessional

Account Executive	Mathematician
Actuary	Medical Assistant
Air Traffic Controller	Metallurgist
Airline Pilot	Mortician
Analyst	Nurse
Auditor	Optician
Biologist	Optometrist
Business Consultant	Osteopath
Chemical Analyst	Paralegal
Chiropractor	Paramedic
Consultant	Paraprofessional
Copilot	Pharmacist
Counselor	Pilot
Dental Assistant	Programmer
Dietician	Projectionist
Drafter	Proofreader
Economist	Psychologist
Engineering Aide	Research Assistant
FBI Agent	Statistician
Flight Engineer	Surveyor
Landscaper	Systems Analyst
Licensed Practical Nurse	Technician
Licensed Vocational Nurse	Therapist

It is convenient if a dictionary is produced in alphabetical order so that individual occupations can be looked up quickly. An example of a few lines of the sort of dictionary that is useful is shown in Figure 39.

Figure 39
Example of Part of *Occupation* Dictionary

Occupation	Attribute
Economist	Semiprofessional
Editor	All Other
Elected Official	Executive
Electrician	Trades
Elevator Operator	Service
Engineer with Degree	Professional
Engineer, Mechanical	Professional
Engineer, Railroad	Service
Engineering Aide	Semiprofessional
Estimator	Office Staff
Examiner	Office Staff
Executive	Executive
Executive Assistant	Manager
Executive Vice President	Executive
Expediter	Office Staff

Each Liaison team will have its own views regarding the classification, both Initial and Classed, of *Occupations*. There is no magic "correct" version; any reasonable classification, particularly if careful attention is paid to the counts of the various possible occupations, will produce effective results.

Let me repeat: *It is essential that the individuals processing the incoming applications use the same classification rules as were used by the manufacturers in developing the scoring system.*

II.2.11.2 Installation Instructions.

When the scoring system is delivered, the user should also be given a document that repeats the decisions that were made in the course of producing the system and reminds the users of the decisions that must be made in order to install the scoring system effectively. Sections II.3 and II.4 discuss the topics that should be included.

II.3 Installation.

Well before the delivery of a scoring system, the user must decide
how it will be operated. Will scoring be done manually or will the
score table be embedded in some way inside a computer? What cut-
off score is to be used? How are credit bureau reports to be handled?
What is to be the policy regarding overriding the recommendations of
the scoring system? Each of these questions, and others discussed in
the following Sections, must be addressed by the user management at
the earliest possible time in the cycle of scoring system development.

II.3.1 Manual or Automatic.

In earlier days, all scoring systems were operated manually. Each
application was scored by hand. If a credit bureau report was to be
acquired, a request for one was made and, when it arrived, the information was incorporated into the final score. Records, if any, were
kept on paper.

Before on-line computers became part of almost every business there
was no practical alternative to manual scoring. There are still cases
where management feels, for one reason or another, that manual
operation is appropriate. However, computers are now well established in the business world and on-line access to them from widely
separated points, both geographically and organizationally, is common. Users now can choose whether to score manually or to embed
scoring in a computer. There are avantages to each, and each has its
problems.

Manual scoring requires extensive staff training. In a nation-wide
organization, such as a finance company with anywhere from 500 to
2,000 offices, there may be as many as four or five people in each
office who will have to understand what a scoring system is and how it
is used. This means that someone will have to train several thousand
people; no trivial task. When one considers the turn-over rate in many
companies, it is clear that the training process is one that needs to go
on indefinitely.

A second problem of manual scoring is the keeping of adequate
records. Records must be kept about how the scoring system is being
operated and how it is performing. Assembling the necessary data
from a manual operation imposes a clerical burden that must be
allowed for. In the United States there are legal requirements for the

retention of documents and for the provision of notices of adverse action when an application is turned down. Every credit grantor must establish procedures to fulfill these requirements, and must be able to demonstrate, if challenged, that they were fulfilled.

In an organization where the credit function is centralized and all applications pass through one office, and where the volume is modest (say under 5,000 per month) a well designed and implemented manual operation can be highly effective.

In organizations where there is any considerable volume of credit applications and operations are centralized, a computer assisted application processing system can save money and improve performance. Even in cases where credit functions are not centralized, the advantages of computer assisted operations are considerable.

It should be noted that the term "Automatic Application Processing" or any of its variants is something of a misnomer, since there is still a manual component even when a computer plays a major part. When a computer is involved, whether the organization is centralized or distributed, terminals are connected to it and application information is entered through them. Once the application information is entered, the computer completes the processing.

During data entry the computer demands that the data entered be formally correct; that is, in fields requiring numbers, numbers must be entered. In fields requiring one of a group of possible entries, any attempted entry outside the permitted group is rejected. In both cases the computer demands a formally correct entry before it will proceed to the next item to be entered.[1]

When data entry is complete and acceptable, the computer applies whatever review rules have been specified by the user or offered by the manufacturer to test the accuracy of the entered data. While we cannot expect to detect all incorrect entries, it is possible to test for the reasonableness of the data that has been inserted. For example, a 19 year old whose entry data says he is a surgeon can be marked for checking. Similarly, an annual income of $250 can trigger a review. Since computers can carry out logical checks of considerable complexity, it is worth the effort to devise them so as to cut down mistakes.

[1] A formally correct entry can, unfortunately, be wrong; an applicant of age 25 can be entered as 52 and the computer has no way of knowing that an error has been made.

On entry the computer can check to see if the application is a duplicate of an application entered during the past several months. It does this by comparing name or address or business address or home or office telephone numbers as well as Social Security numbers. Cases are known of individuals who submit several applications with slightly differing information hoping that at least one of them will get through. The detection and investigation of such attempts can reduce fraud losses. Other possible frauds are reduced by comparing each new application with lists of information stored in the computer about known previous frauds.[1]

Once the general acceptability of the entered information is established and no match is made with any previous application or with the file of known frauds, the application is scored. If the score triggers a request for a credit report, it is automatically requested from the appropriate bureau without operator intervention. Also without operator intervention, the returned credit bureau report is scored and the final score for the application is determined. If the application is to be accepted an appropriate entry is made in the file of new accounts, which the opens a new account in the master file and causes a card to be issued.

If the application is to be rejected, the computer automatically produces the Adverse Action letter (in the U.S., where it is required by law, and elsewhere if management policy so specifies). If there is an exception to be made as the result of the action of some review rule, the application, along with the score and the credit bureau report, is sent to a reviewer for the final decision.

Once the final action is taken, the data from the application and the bureau report are filed for later use in reports and for the archives.

Using a computer to process applications for credit has many advantages. When all of the steps after data entry are carried out by a machine, processing is fast. Second, the number of errors, while not eliminated, is reduced. Third, duplications and many possibly fraudulent applications can be detected, avoiding the heavy losses that such accounts can cause. Fourth, record keeping is automatic and all the data are available for almost all of the reports that are useful for the management of a credit scoring system. Finally, management can be assured that the requirements for Adverse Action notification are met

---

[1]Since there are legal problems whenver fraud is suspected, be sure to have a careful legal review of all procedures in this area.

according to the instructions of its own legal staff.

While many organizations operate their scoring systems manually, I strongly suspect that in the next few years we will see more and more automated operations.

Computer aided scoring can be done in a variety of ways. At one extreme is a stand-alone computer dedicated exclusively to operating the scoring system and all of its associated functions and, at the other, the scoring is implanted into the organization's own data processing system. Each, naturally, has advantages and disadvantages.

The stand-alone machine with its suite of programs has the advantage that it can be purchased by the credit department independent of any other department of the organization. It can specify what the machine is to do without having to coordinate its operation with other departments. Consequently, it can install a machine and go into operation considerably more rapidly than when the requirements have to be made a part of the budget process of the entire organization.

In addition, a stand-alone machine is dedicated entirely to scoring and is under the complete control of its users. The credit department does not have to stand in line with everyone else to get a program written or tested. Most of the changes that will be wanted can be made by the credit staff by taking advantage of the "user friendliness" of the programs. Since a stand-alone machine does not share its time with other organizational functions, its response is usually quicker than when it shares access with other operations.

The principal disadvantage of the stand alone machine is that it normally does not have easy access to the actual performance of the accounts once they are on the books, so that it cannot, by itself, collect information on the performance of the system. As a result, the preparation of reports on delinquency and the collection of information that will be needed when the time comes to replace the scoring system must rely on other parts of the organization.

The obvious advantage of having the scoring system a part of the general data processing facility is that separate equipment, with its support and maintenance requirements, is not needed. Furthermore, with score easily placed in the customer master record, it is possible to evaluate the scoring system (that is, tabulate portfolo performance by score) on an on-going basis.

The current disadvantage of making scoring part of the general data processing facility is that it has to take its place in the development queue. This process may inject an unacceptable delay in the initial development and the later modification of the application processing operation. However, this is likely to be a temporary difficulty, since data processing systems are becoming easier to manage and more amenable to the demands of multiple users.

Software has been developed that can be installed in an organization's data processing system with a maximum of compatibility and with little demand on the data processing staff. In addition, this software is specifically designed so that it can be modfied freely over a wide range without any change in the manner in which it interfaces with the other operations of the data processing function, allowing much of the programming to be done by the credit staff without having to call for any contribution from the data processing department.

II.3.2 Cut-off Score.

The cut-off score is the score below which no application will be approved and at or above which applications will be recommended for approval. Clearly, this decision must be made before the scoring system can be put into operation.

In theory, the setting of the optimum cut-off score is a simple matter. If the net profit from a Good account is known, and the net loss from a Bad account is also known, then it is simple to calculate the number of Good accounts that are necessary to offset the loss from one Bad account. This quotient defines the odds at which the incremental gain is equal to the incremental loss, and the score associated with those odds is the appropriate cut-off score.

In practice things are not quite so simple. The true profit from a Good account and the true loss from a Bad account are very difficult to determine. In fact, I don't know of any organization that has even tried to do it. Even if a reasonable guess as to their values can be made, the resulting cut-off score may still be uncertain. If a credit department is a profit center, then it must operate at a profit or, at worst, without loss. In that case the reasoning given above may be adequate to set the cut-off score.

If, however, the credit department is considered part of an overall operation including merchandizing and customer service, determining the "overall profit" from a Good account and the "overall loss" from a Bad account, is made more difficult because the value of goodwill is not easily quantified in a way that will get the concurrence of all of the parties concerned.

In the real world, it is usually found undesirable to subject an organization to sudden and drastic changes, no matter how well founded such shifts might be. If a credit department has an acceptance rate of, say, 60%, it would be a bold manager indeed who would install scoring with a cut-off that produced either a 40% or an 80% acceptance rate.

Prudence suggests that a scoring system initially be installed with a cut-off that delivers an acceptance rate that is close to, if not equal to, the rate before installation. Alternatively, it might be possible to use a cut-off score that holds losses constant while enjoying an increase in volume. These cases are illustrated in Figures 35 and 36 in Section II.2.10. A third alternative is a cut-off score between these two end points; a cut-off outside these limits is asking a great deal from a management about to undertake the use of a tool with which they have no experience.

When experience has been gained and the performance of the scoring system has earned the confidence of management, it is much easier to make a shift in the cut-off score to a value better calculated to achieve management's goals.

II.3.3   Use of Credit Bureau information.

As discussed above in Section II.2.9, it is not uncommon to develop a scoring table in which the credit bureau information is marginal to the information contained on the application. In such cases it may be possible to reach a decision on the basis of the information on an application without going to the trouble and expense of acquiring a credit bureau report. If a score on application data alone is so low that, no matter how good a credit report is and how many points it would earn, the final total would still not be up to the cut-off, acquiring a credit bureau report is a waste of time and money. Similarly, if the score from the application information is so high that no matter how many negative points are merited from a bad credit report the final score would still be over the cut-off, then here again getting a credit bureau report is a waste of time and money.

The scoring table shown in Figure 31 illustrates these cases. The most points that an applicant can get from the credit bureau information is 18. Therefore, if an applicant is awarded a total that is 19 points below the cut-off score from all of the other characteristics, even if that applicant were to be awarded 18 points from credit bureau information, he would still be one point below cut-off and the application would be declined. In such a case buying a credit report is a waste of money, since it will not affect the decision.[1]

At the other extreme is an application that gets 15 or more points over the cut-off. In such a case, even if the credit report merits a negative 15 points, the final total will still be at the cut-off or higher, again making the bureau report superfluous.

A note of caution should be sounded here. Many, if not most, credit managers find it difficult to accept an application, no matter how high its score, if the credit report is seriously negative. In most of the cases in my experience, credit managers are quite willing to save the money on the low scoring applications that cannot achieve the cut-off no matter what the report may say (although there are not a few who find even this difficult), but they decline to go along with the idea that an applicant should be accepted if the score is high enough to overcome the worst possible credit report.

This is a reasonable enough attitude. While it may burden the organization with some additional expense, it does provide the manager, who is, after all, the responsible individual, with additional confidence in the operation of his own department. Management can conduct experiments that will help in this area, as will be discussed in Section II.4.4 .

---

[1] When a scoring system is newly installed it is not uncommon to hear a request for an exception for an application "only one little point" under the cut-off. If that exception is granted, what will happen to an application that is two points under the cut-off, or now only one point under, since the exception effectively lowered the cut-off by one point. A cut-off is a cut-off.

II.3.4 Overrides.

An override is a decision by a credit department to take an action that is contrary to the recommendation of the scoring system. High side overrides are accounts that are turned down even though their scores are at the cut-off or higher, and low side overrides are accounts that are accepted even though the score is below the cut-off.[1]

There are three basic types of overrides; informational, policy, and intuitional. They are very different in their nature and in the way they should be viewed in relation to a credit scoring system. Management must establish rules for each type.

First, informational overrides. In these cases the decision recommended by the score is reversed because an evaluator is in possession of information that had no part in the construction of the scoring table or that is peculiar to a specific individual. The obvious example is an application that scores very well but the applicant has just gone to jail. In such a case it is not unreasonable to decline to grant the requested credit; in fact, it would be irresponsible not to do so.

An example at the other end is an application that scores below the cut-off where the evaluator knows that the applicant has just obtained a new job, since submitting the application, with an income that, had it been scored, would have put the final score over the cut-off. Here again it makes sense to reverse the recommendation of the scoring system and to accept the application.

Informational overrides, while they make perfectly good sense, are rare. It is a rare occasion indeed when a credit evaluator recognizes the identity of the individual whose application he has in hand and also just happens to have information about that specific applicant that is sufficient to warrant the reversal of the scoring system recommendation. ★

However rare they may be, they can still happen, and a credit department is well advised to make provision for such a possibility. In every case a written record of the facts should be made, including the reason for the override. In the case of the applications that are

---

[1]I am not talking about blanket rejects or accepts that make no reference to a score; in fact they are decided without any score being calculated. Blanket rejects might apply to applications from outside the business area covered by the enterprise or to applicants under 18 years of age. Blanket accepts might include company officers and members of their families.

accepted despite low scores, the records can be reviewed later to see how they performed, as the score predicted or as the overrider predicted.

Policy overrides occur when management sets up special rules for some kinds of applications. In general, policy overrides act to accept applications that would be turned down on the basis of score alone. If an enterprise decides to encourage an applicant group not previously solicited, management may decide to grant that group an extra 10 points or so for some interval of time. For example, if management decides that the students at the local university might prove a long term source of good business even if they are unlikely to achieve a score high enough on the basis of their current status, management might grant them extra points in the hope of developing loyal customers.

A policy override that is often treated rather casually is the case where an applicant is granted credit despite a low scoring application on the grounds that he is a good customer in some other area. This is most commonly the case with bank credit cards where the bank is unwilling to turn down an applicant who has an account with the bank. Here again, this is not an unreasonable position to take. However, the override should not be automatic, it should be made within a considered and explicit policy established by management and not be something that each credit evaluator can apply according to his own feelings.

A bank relationship may take many forms. An individual can have a personal checking account with a small balance or be the president of a corporation that keeps millions in the bank. It is wise to consider these two carefully, as well as the many other possible relationships that may exist and to devise a policy to cover them all. For example, it might be decided by management that in the case of a business account over one million dollars that has been in place for some time, credit cards should be granted to any officer of that business who applies for one.[1] Similarly, management might decide that a business account of a hundred thousand dollars up to one million would allow a policy override only for the president of the business but not any

---

[1] This sounds simple enough, but like many business decisions, has hidden dangers. What happens when the officer changes jobs? If he has paid well, there is no great problem, but if he is delinquent, what is to be done? In fact, how is the credit grantor even going to find out that the officer is no longer an employee of the company to which the courtesy of unevaluated credit was extended.

other officer or employee. Further, a business account of under one hundred thousand dollars might be designated by management to award, say, 15 points extra to any officer and 5 points to any other employee.

Policy override rules can be established for personal accounts as well. In every case management should decide exactly how many points are to be awarded to applicants with various types of bank relationships.

Another source of policy overrides is third party pressure. For example, automobile dealers have no small leverage with lending institutions and, from time to time, have been known to pressure them to grant an automobile loan to an applicant who scores well below the cut-off, as a reward for all the business sent to that lender. Here again the override should not be automatic.

Management should examine the entire portfolio of loans provided by that dealer to decide just how valuable he is to the lender. That evaluation will permit the lender to assign a number of points to that lender that are to be applied when an exception is requested. If it is decided that a particular dealer can have an extra 17 points assigned to an applicant, if he requests it, it must be understood that an applicant will still be turned down if, after including the extra 17 points, the score is not up to the cut-off.

Management must decide if it is willing to take the risk of losing that dealer as a source of business and assign points on that basis. It would be wise to discuss this with the dealer so that the grounds for exceptions are known to both parties.

The third type of override is the intuitional override It is the most common and the least justified. It is an intuitional override when an evaluator reverses the decision recommended by the score for reasons other than policy or information. This reversal is usually made, on the rejection side, when the evaluator decides that the application before him is "weak" for some reason that he cannot explain; his judgment and experience tell him that it would be unwise to accept that application.

A reverse case is also possible; an application can be considered "strong" despite a score that is below the cut-off. In both cases the evaluator cannot explain his decision other than to claim conviction based on experience. In fact the evaluator is saying that his experience, applied to that particular application, is better than the bottled experience of the organization as manifested by the scoring system.

For reasons that I cannot understand, most credit managements permit their evaluators to make intuitional overrides on a very liberal basis. Some managements give evaluators specific authority to override the scoring system within five or ten points of the cut-off score. This is the least justifiable policy that can be followed. It is precisely in the neighborhood of the cut-off that a scoring system is most valuable. It is not difficult to decide to grant credit to an applicant who scores 100 points over the cut-off or to decline it to an applicant who scores 100 points below it; it is close to the cut-off that credit scoring systems prove their worth.

Some justification for permitting intuitional overrides can be found in the idea that the evaluators will be without any true evaluative function if they merely follow the recommendation of the scoring table. In order to maintain the morale of these individuals, they are permitted to override the system.

This is an empty argument; the traditional task of the credit evaluator disappears when a scoring system in in operation; that is the whole point of the scoring system. The only decision concerns applications that trigger a review according to the rules established by management. If there is *information* available to an evaluator, then he should apply the rules regarding informational overrides. If there is a *policy*, the evaluator should apply it.

It would be wise to re-title the position to remove any word that sounds like "analyst" or "evaluator"; there is no analysis or evaluation called for when a scoring system is in place. The only decision to be made is whether or not an observable, objective condition exists that merits the application of an informational or a policy override.

Reality intrudes here as it does in other areas of human endeavor. Managers are rightly unwilling to damage the morale of their staffs at the time a new tool is installed and before that tool has demonstrated its worth. Permitting intuitional overrides is a reasonable procedure at the time of the initiation of a credit scoring system.

What is not reasonable is the indefinite continuation of this permission without examination. A sensible course is to keep adequate records of all types of overrides so that the performance of those that were accepted despite low scores can be tracked. These records should show the score, the identity of the individual making the override, and any reason given by the evaluator for the override. As time passes and the accounts mature, it will be found that the accounts accepted with scores below cut-off perform as their scores predicted, not as the overriders predicted. At that time management should take action to diminish or eliminate intuitional overrides.

Intuitional overrides are also used to turn down accounts scoring over the cut-off. These, too, can be expected to perform as their scores indicate, and management should act to diminish or to eliminate these as well. Experiments to evaluate intuitional overrides are discussed in Section II.4.4, below.

II.3.5 Credit Limit or Loan Amount.

In the manufacture of most credit scoring systems Good and Bad accounts are defined as those that perform satisfactorily or unsatifactorily, respectively, to the lender, without any consideration given to the credit limit or the amount of the original loan.[1] As a result, the credit score is not a ruler that is marked off in dollars; the user should not use score as the sole basis for the assignment of credit limit.

Every credit grantor has a policy on credit limits long before scoring is installed. In some cases everyone gets the same credit limit, in others the credit limit depends on something that is known about the applicant. There is no reason to change this policy just because a scoring system has been installed. On the contrary, since the scoring system was developed based on a population that was granted credit limits according to the current policy, there is every reason to maintain it.[2]

II.3.6 Applicant Information Verification.

Policies regarding how and what information is to be verified are enormously varied. There are, doubtless, still creditors who verify things like claimed bank accounts, and even do so by mail, as was not

---

[1] Throughout this section I will use "credit limit" alone, but the reference is also to the amount of a loan in those cases where it is applicable.

[2] This discussion refers only to the initial credit limit assigned to an accepted applicant. The manner in which score can be used to modify credit limits after an account has been in operation for some interval is discussed in Part III of this book.

uncommon 25 years ago. At the other extreme there are many credit grantors who do no checking whatever in the interest of rapid response to customer interest.

Here again, as in the case of credit limits, the scoring system that is delivered was based on a sample of accounts that were opened under whatever verification policy was in existence when the sample data came on the books. There is no reason to modify that policy just because a scoring system has been installed.

If the policy in place involves any verification whatever, once the scoring system is in operation verification should be postponed until after an application has been scored, since if the score recommends that it be rejected there is no longer any need to verify any of the data.

II.3.7 Security.

There is good reason to keep the details of the scoring system from becoming public knowledge.[1] Each user will have to decide who is to have access to the score card and what steps are to be taken to protect it. If a scoring system is to be embedded inside a computer, security is not much of a problem, since the table is available in full detail only to the management staff that implants it.[2] My experience has been that, aside from the occasional criminally inclined employee, most of the people connected with the operation of a scoring system guard it carefully.

II.3.8 Use of Information Other Than Application Data.

There are many cases, particularly in banks, where an applicant for a credit card may do business with the bank in areas other than the

---

[1] I have always wondered what would happen if a scoring system were made public; how many fraudulent applicants would appear. So far no lender has been willing to try to find out, although several have had "score yourself" applications used to increase volume. Careful examination of such applications shows that practically everyone "passes" and is then asked to fill in "a few simple items" which turn out to be a standard application which will be evaluated in the normal manner and which can result in a rejection. I haven't seen one of these lately, so I conclude that the public was not impressed.

[2] This is not strictly true, since a determined data entry operator could experiment by making small changes in a fictitious application and note the resulting changes in the score that was achieved. However, I have never heard that this has been done although there have been cases of deliberately fraudulent applications (with attributes that are obviously going to score well) entered by employees with consequent losses by the enterprise.

credit card. If this information is not elicited on the application but the bank has access to it in some other way, management will have to decide how to handle it. This is a subject that has already been discussed under "Overrides" in Section II.3.4, above, but a few additional comments are in order.

If the bank operates its credit card in the same geographical area as the one from which it draws its other customers, it is possible that an applicant will have some other business relationship with the bank. If this is the case, "Other Bank Relationships" should be a Characteristic recorded on the development sample data and thus be eligible for entry into the scoring system as it is being constructed.

Before single master files of customers were available it was not easy to associate a credit card application with any other business relationship with the bank. In addition to developing an override policy in this regard, management should take advantage of gradually improving data management within the organization and should begin to collect the "Other Bank Relationship" data so that statistics can be gathered on the value of that information in predicting credit card behavior.

There are ways that such independently gathered information can be appended to a scoring table without having to go back to the beginning and starting all over.

If, on the other hand, the area covered by the bank in its credit card operation is larger than the area from which its "regular" customers are obtained, then there is less chance that a particular applicant will have some other bank relationship. In such cases it might be worth the trouble to note the address of the applicant and if it is within the bank's "normal" area, check for some other bank relationship (which is fairly easy when direct access to basic information is available) and apply a specific override policy to such cases.

II.3.9 Education.

By "Education" I mean telling the organization what it should know so that scoring can become an effective management tool. There are three major groups in the enterprise to be considered: those directly involved in the credit function, management, and everyone else.

For scoring to be effective, the staff of the credit department has got to have confidence that it is sound. If scoring is new to the company there will be many opinions and many attitudes, and some of them may be hostile to scoring. The organization is well advised to take the time and trouble to explain scoring to the credit staff and to answer, as far as is possible, the criticisms that may be raised.

Established credit departments that are new to scoring have every right to claim that they have done their jobs well in the past and to doubt that a process that does not make use of their experience and judgment cannot do as well as they can.[1] While they have a right to make these claims, they are wrong, and it is up to management to provide a specific demonstration that this is so. The time it takes to lay out the scoring system and its development will be well spent.

Other than the fact that it takes time to do it, I can think of no reason for not discussing the development of the scoring system in detail. Every step in the process should be discussed to show that each is based on the experience of the enterprise and that the data that are used all come from the files of the credit department. The manner in which the Initial Enumeration is done, and the actual results of that enumeration should be shown to the staff and discussed with them. ★

In many cases in my experience, the staff are most interested in these figures, finding justification for some of their opinions in the counts of real cases and adjusting long held opinions when faced with actual counts of their own data. The process of classing should also be discussed, as well as the final score table.

Scoring education of the credit department should start as soon as the decision is made to acquire a scoring system. The greater part the staff has in the development of the system, the better they will understand it. If they are involved in the development from the very beginning, being part of the sample gathering process and being kept informed about the progress of the system by the liaison team, as well as being encouraged to contribute ideas and opinions, they will be far more likely to accept the system and to use it well.

Some organizations that plan to implant the score card in a computer prefer not to reveal the actual score values to the staff on security grounds, but I think this is an error. To allow the staff to develop

[1] Incidentally, the claim that the experience of the staff is being ignored is quite wrong; it is exactly that experience that produced the information that was used to construct the scoring system. The scoring system builds on that data, formalizes the process and improves the results.

confidence in the system they will have to see it work. One of the best ways to do this is to let the staff score (manually, even if the final installation is to be in a computer) a group of current delinquent accounts.

It will be discovered in this process that many of these delinquents (accounts that the staff had accepted) would have been rejected had the scoring system been available at the time these individuals applied.

Scoring some satisfactory accounts will also show that the scoring system would have approved them. Even scoring some of the rejects is helpful, since I have seen it lead to such comments as "Why did we turn this one down; it looks OK to me" in cases where the score turns out to be over the cut-off. The majority of the rejects will be shown to score below the cut-off. This is an effective confidence-building demonstration.

The credit department should make every effort to try to answer any criticisms that individuals may have. Manufacturers can be expected to give every assistance they can in this process since it is in their interest to have a successful installation.

In particular, the problem of overriding should be gone into in some detail. An organization may decide to permit rather extensive overriding early in the life of the scoring system if it is faced with any degree of opposition to scoring from the staff that is in place. If it does so, however, it should make clear that override permission is being given so that the credit staff can find out for itself that the overrides do not accomplish the goal that they are intended to achieve. Records must be kept so that this demonstration can be made based on actual data.

In the end, the credit staff must understand that the use of the scoring system is not optional; it is the policy of the company to use scoring and that overrides are permitted only within the rules established by credit management. It must be made clear that subversion of the scoring system is a dischargeable offence. Subversion is not only a willful violation of company policy, but will make it difficult, if not impossible, to determine whether or not the scoring system is working.

One of the groups of management that must be fully educated about scoring is the legal department. They must be involved in the development of the system from the beginning and must review the proposed manner of operation with great care. As mentioned earlier, there should be legal representation on the Liaison team, if possible. In particular, the legal staff must be made aware, if it is not already, of the legal requirements surrounding credit scoring. For systems in the U.S., this applies particularly to the use of the Characteristic *Age*, if it appears in the scoring system, and to the manner in which notices of adverse action are produced and transmitted, both of these being subjects covered by law and regulation.

The manner and extent of the education of management senior to the credit department is a matter for the head of that department to decide. Some scoring matters affect parts of the organization outside the credit department. Care should be taken that the impact of scoring on these other parts of the company is known before these effects are felt. In particular, this refers to things like company policies that might act to override the scoring system. For example, it must be understood, in cases where company officers and their families are automatically granted credit, that these accounts, whether they prove good or bad at some later date, are not to be included in the data used to evaluate the effectiveness of the scoring system.

Another problem that affects more than one department arises when an applicant has some business relationship with the company in addition to the request for credit. All the parties that can be involved in such problems must understand what the scoring system is and must contribute to the manner in which conflicts can be resolved. This problem has already been discussed in Sections II.3.4 and II.3.8.

Education of the staff of the enterprise not connected directly with credit and not involved on a management level is a subject that each organization will decide for itself. In organizations with internal news letters, an article on scoring is often found helpful, particularly to those employees who are likely to be asked questions about how credit is evaluated. Customers frequently ask bank tellers how they should fill in their credit card applications, so it is helpful for these tellers to have some information about scoring.

II.3.10 Training.

In addition to the basic education discussed in the previous section, the staff that will be directly involved in scoring has to be trained in its use. Whether scoring is to be done manually or will be implanted in a computer, the whole process for the operation of the scoring function must be designed with care, and people must be trained to take their parts in it.

When scoring is done manually consideration must be given to how the existing application flow is to be modified. Where in the flow will scoring take place? Who is to do the scoring? What records will be kept of the score and the action taken? At the very least a record should be kept of the number of applications received, the scores they achieved (both before and after a credit report is acquired if scoring is a two stage procedure), and whether each was accepted or rejected. It would also be wise (especially in the U.S.) to record that an Adverse Action notice was sent to all declined applicants.

Once these decisions have been made and the personnel who are going to do the actual scoring are identified, they need basic education in what scoring is all about, and they must be shown how applications are scored and how the required records are kept.

The easiest way to do this is to develop a body of applications that are correctly scored that the trainees can use for practice. Some of these are scored as a group effort with discussion of each item, and the rest are done by each of the trainees separately. The results of these individually scored applications are then discussed, with explanations being given of all discrepancies.

This training process should continue until the trainers are confident that the trainees have a good command of the process and know when and how to ask questions when an application shows up that they are not sure how to score.

When scoring is to be done by a computer, the application information still has to be entered correctly. This is principally a matter of explaining the coding instructions so that the data entry operators have a clear grasp of how coding is done and why it is done in the manner required by their particular scoring system.

There are many organizations where scoring is done or data are entered at many different places. In these cases there are many people, perhaps thousands, who must be trained. Training is then a full time process and the enterprise will have to organize a training staff. I am familiar with cases where an organization sent a score table out in the mail and instructed the local offices to use it without training or any instruction whatever. This is a blueprint for a failure. If an organization is unwilling to provide the necessary training, it might be wiser to stay away from scoring altogether. When an organization decides to acquire a scoring system, one of the components of that decision must be an understanding of the cost of training and a willingness to accept that cost as part of the investment.

Large organizations should consider the preparation of video taped instruction materials. Some of these can cover the basic educational needs of the organization and some can go into the details of scoring, however it is to be done in that particular organization. None of the manufacturers of scoring systems has yet produced a generic educational video, which is a shame since it would meet a strong need. However, in addition to a generic item, it would be necessary to have additional material especially produced for each particular organization, both for general education and for training in the practice of scoring. Video production is becoming cheaper every day, so I hope that organizations will begin to use video training in the not too distant future.

II.3.11 Notice of Adverse Action.

In the United States the law requires that when an applicant is denied credit in the terms understood by the application, the applicant must be provided with a notice of adverse action. Section 701(d)(2) of Title VII of Public Law 93-495 states, in pertinent part:

> Each applicant against whom adverse action is taken
> shall be entitled to a statement of reasons for such
> action from the creditor.

Since I am not a lawyer and, therefore, unqualified to provide legal advice, I will offer none. The legal department of any organization granting credit, with or without a credit scoring system, should make sure that the procedures followed by the credit department are in accordance with their understanding of the law in this area.

Other countries may have other regulations regarding credit in general or scoring in particular, so legal staffs should make sure that all its credit activities are suitable.

II.4 Operation.

As soon as a scoring system is in operation, its management will want to know how it is working and how the performance of the scoring system compares with that of the system it replaced. Unfortunately, there is no quick answer to this. It takes some months for enough scored accounts to go on the books and be there long enough to show either Good or Bad performance. If accounts have a fairly long average lifetime, say three to five years, it will take from 18 months to over two years before even half of the total portfolio consists of scored accounts.[1] It might take six months to a year for enough data to accumulate. ★

While a definitive comparison between the old and the new method cannot be made close to the time of the installation of the scoring system, it is possible to make various measurements that will give management some confidence that the system is working as expected.

An absolute comparison of the previous system with scoring is never possible when the previous system has been turned off. However, in an organization like a finance company with many offices, a nose-to-nose test can be conducted by installing scoring in some offices and leaving the original procedure in the others. If the two groups of offices have been chosen carefully and are reasonably comparable, a comparison of the effectiveness of the two systems can be made. When scoring is installed company wide all at once and the previous system is abandoned no comparison can be made that is as definitive as a parallel test.

If scoring is installed company wide all at once, which is usually the practice nowadays, the first and quickest test that can be made is to determine the reject rate as soon as possible and to monitor it on a continuing basis. The point here is to make sure that the selected cut-off score is producing the expected reject rate. The rate can be determined by hand-counting the accepts and rejects and comparing the resulting reject rate with that predicted by the scoring system.

A better method is to establish a formal score recording procedure. If scoring is done in a computer this can be done by a program on an on-going basis. In a manual operation, each scorer should keep a running

---

[1] This is not peculiar to scoring. Any major change in application processing policy cannot be evaluated until the portfolio contains enough accounts accepted under the new policy so that meaningful conclusions can be drawn.

tally of his work on a form such as is shown in Figure 40.

Figure 40

Scoring Tally Sheet		
Name of Scorer: J. Smith		
Dates Covered: From Feb. 5 To Feb. 11		
Score Interval	Accepts	Rejects
Below 160		
160 - 169		卌 ||
170 - 179		卌 |
180 - 184		卌 卌 ||||
185 - 189		卌 卌 |||
190 - 194	|||	卌 卌 卌 ||||
195 - 199	||||	卌 卌 卌
200 - 204	卌 卌 卌 卌 ||	|||
205 - 209	卌 卌 卌 卌	||||
210 - 214	卌 卌 卌 ||||	|
215 - 219	卌 卌 卌 卌 ||	
220 - 224	卌 卌 卌 ||	
225 - 229	卌 卌 卌 |||	
230 - 239	卌 卌 卌 ||	
240 - 249	卌 卌 卌 卌 |	
250 and Over	卌 卌 卌 卌 卌	
Totals	193	82

This form also shows the number of overrides made by any scorer, a figure that is most important for effective scoring system management. If the cut-off score for the system is at 200 points, every tally mark below 200 in the Accept column represents an override. Similarly, every tally mark at 200 or above in the Reject column also represents an override.

A separate report should be prepared listing every override, the reason for it, and the identity of the individual making it. Periodically, the performance of the override accounts that were accepted below the cut-off should be examined. It will be found that the override accounts behave much as the score predicted, that is, at an unacceptable rate of delinquency. When this is made clear management can make a strong case to reduce overrides. In the unlikely event that the override accounts perform better than expected, a situation I have never encountered, management can try to find out what it was that led to the overrides and to benefit from that knowledge.

Development Time Validation. At the time of the development of the scoring system, the manufacturer may withhold part of the sample data of Goods and Bads for use in testing the power of the scoring system, what is known as Development Time Validation. As soon as the system has been developed, this withheld sample is scored. The mean score of the Goods and the mean score of the Bads are determined and their difference is calculated. This difference measures the strength of the scoring system and can be compared with the similar figure for the development sample. These are usually extremely close, showing that the developed scores act as expected on a separate body of Good and Bad accounts.

A further validation can be made by scoring a body of accounts that were not in the original sample.[1] If possible they should be newer accounts whose Good or Bad performance became known after the original development sample was taken. This new group of Goods and Bads must be assembled using the same rules as were used when the original sample was collected. These are scored, as before, and the difference between the mean of the Goods and the mean of the Bads is determined. Once again, it will be found that this difference is very close to that of the original sample and, therefore, that the strength of the scoring system has not diminished.

It is, of course, possible that the new scores and the original ones may not demonstrate close correspondence; validation may fail. In such a case it is up to the manufacturers to produce a scoring system that does validate. Fortunately, I have no experience with a non-validating scoring system and have heard of only one or two out of the many thousands that have been produced.

As the fraction of accounts on the books that were scored begins to become appreciable, various other reports can be produced that demonstrate the effectiveness of the scoring system, as will be discussed in Section II.4.1, below.

---

[1]Validation can be carried out using only 300 or so Good and Bad accounts since validation calculates only the mean scores of the two groups. Larger samples are required in developing the scoring system since it involves calculation of score points for many attributes of many characteristics.

II.4.1 Reports.

II.4.1.1 Monitoring.

As soon as the operation of a scoring system has started, the user must ensure that scoring and data entry are being done correctly. It is not unusual for many errors to be made as the staff learns how to score. Errors should be detected as quickly as possible so that training in scoring can cut them down. Checking for scoring errors is called Monitoring, and consists of having an expert coder re-score applications (or re-enter application data, if the system operates through a computer) and compare the re-scored results with the originals.

I know of cases where over 50% of the applications were scored incorrectly during the start up of a scoring system.[1] It is important to reduce the error rate to 5% or less as quickly as possible. If monitoring is done on an on-going basis the organization can expect the error rate to fall rapidly and to remain at an acceptable level.

One of the common errors made by scorers new to the task is to pay too little attention to the attributes of the Characteristic *Occupation*, when it is in the system. When this happens, the scorers tend to have incomplete knowledge of the occupations that fall into each category and, rather than look up a new one when it appears, they simply mark it "All Other". A count of the number of "All Other" tallys compared with the number in the original system statistics will show if this is taking place.

II.4.1.2 Population Stability.

Users must keep track of the nature of the population. Is the population of current applicants similar to the one on which the scoring system was developed? If the population of current applicants is very different from the original population, the scoring system is liable to be less effective than expected. Many factors can cause the incoming population of applicants to change. Credit operations frequently seek

---

[1] This does not mean that accounts that should be rejected will be accepted or that accounts that should be accepted will be rejected 50% of the time. It means that some error will be made in calculating the score although only a few of these will result in a wrong decision. However, even a few are too many and everything possible should be done to minimize or, if possible, eliminate scoring errors. Scoring errors, even those that do not result in a wrong decision, will negatively affect the records and make it harder to evaluate the scoring system.

to expand their coverage and do so by seeking customers in geographical areas other than those providing the population on which the scoring system was built.

Credit grantors also may seek to attract sub-populations not previously sought. For example, a credit grantor may decide to solicit membership of college students, or employees at some major industry, or members of some fraternal or service association. All of these new sub-populations may cause a scoring system built on a different population to diminish in effectiveness.

A third source of population variation is changes in the strength of the general economy. If an economy suffers either a recession or an expansion, the number of individuals seeking credit may change (in either direction) and the demographics of the applicant population may change along with the number.

While it is certainly not an inevitable consequence of the expansion of the applicant population that a scoring system will diminish in power, it is essential that the population be followed so that departures from expectation in the performance of the scoring system can be anticipated.

The Population Stability Report compares the scores achieved by the current population with those of the population on which the system was developed. The more closely these two sets of scores compare, the closer the new population is to the original population.

It will be recalled that, when the scoring system is being developed, the goal is to make the mean of the distribution of the scores of the Good accounts be as far as possible from the mean of the distribution of the Bad accounts. The measure of the power of the scoring system is the amount of separation between the means of the Good and the Bad distributions, as is discussed in Section II.2.9 and Figure 25. In trying to find out how closely the current population resembles the original, we now want just the reverse; we would like the distribution of the current scores to be as close as possible to that of the original population. The closer together these curves are, the greater the degree of confidence that the system can be expected to operate as planned.

Figure 41 shows a plot of the distribution of scores of the population used to develop a scoring system compared with the distributions of scores of two other populations, one very similar to the original and one quite different from it.[1] If a user finds the distribution of scores close together like the two on the left in Figure 41, he can be confident that the population has not changed. On the other hand, if the two curves are separated, as are the curve marked "Original Population" and the curve marked "Changed Population", it would be wise to seek an explanation of the change and then to take whatever action might be called for.

Figure 41

Comparison of Distributions of Scores of
Development Sample and Current Applications

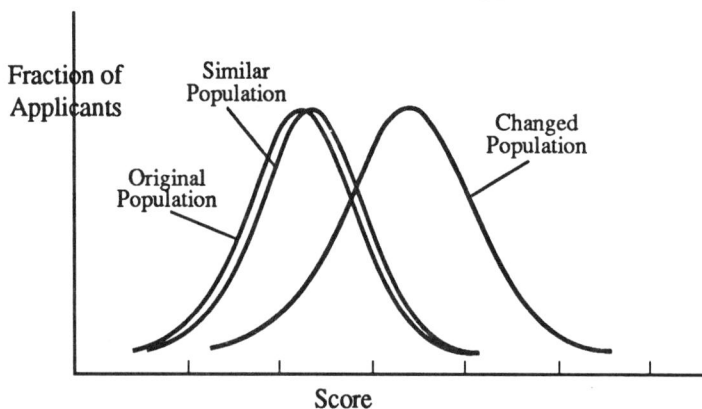

II.4.1.3 Validation.

A scoring system must be validated as time goes on. The procedure used at development time can no longer be used, since the performance of applicants being turned down cannot be known. However, the accepted accounts can be rank ordered by score. If such an ordering shows that the higher the score, the higher the odds for satisfactory performance, it is reasonable to conclude that the system remains effective. This is discussed below in Section II.4.1.5

II.4.1.4 Characteristic Analysis Report.

The Characteristic Analysis Report compares, for each Characteristic, the percentages of current applicants that fall into the various Attributes with the percentages that fell into these same Attributes when the scoring system was developed. An example of the sort of report that can be produced is shown in Figure 42. Even without any mathemati-

[1]For a slightly more detailed discussion of Population Stability, see the Appendix.

Figure 42

Sample of Part of a Characteristic Analysis
Report Showing Population Changes

Occupation	% of Original Population	% of Current Population
Retired	10	10
Professional	20	10
Clerical	35	10
Sales	15	21
Service	10	31
All Other	10	15
Blank	5	5

cal analysis, it is clear that there has been a change in the population. There are now more Sales and Service applicants and fewer Professional and Clerical applicants than there were in the population on which the scoring system was developed. Somewhat more precise is a numerical analysis of the difference, which is shown in the Appendix.

A Characteristic Analysis Report has value by itself, but it is even more useful whenever the Population Stability shows that the current population is markedly different from the original one and the user wants to know where those differences lie.

II.4.1.5 Report on Delinquency by Score and Exposure.

If the applicant and customer populations are reasonably stable, the general performance of a scoring system can be examined through a report that shows the delinquency of the entire portfolio by score. In its simplest form it is merely a table that shows the rate of delinquency for each score interval from low to high, as illustrated in Figure 43.

This basic table shows one important fact but conceals too many others to be truly useful. It demonstrates that the scoring system is performing, since it shows that delinquency decreases as score goes up, the basic claim of a scoring system. However, since it puts all delinquents together, those a few days late and those over 90 days late, and because it includes those that came on the books during the past month and cannot possibly have yet become delinquent, the results can be misleading.

Figure 43

Basic Table of Delinquency by Score

Score Interval	% Delinquent
Below 170	36.8
170-179	16.4
180-189	15.7
190-199	17.2
200-204	10.2
205-209	8.9
210-214	8.6
215-219	6.8
220-224	6.7
225-229	6.7
230-239	3.5
240 and Over	2.3
Overall	9.2

For a Delinquency by Score report to be useful it should deal only with accounts that have been on the books about the same length of time and which, therefore, have all had the same exposure to the possibility of delinquency. Figure 44 shows a Delinquency by Score table for accounts that have been on the books from 12 to 15 months, and where delinquency is defined in the same way as Bad accounts were defined when the scoring system was developed. ★ Figure 44 continues to show that delinquency goes down as score goes up. Similar tables can be constructed for accounts that have been on the

Figure 44

90 Day + Delinquency by Score for Accounts on the Books
12 - 15 Months

Score Interval	% Delinquent
Below 170	17.4
170-179	11.6
180-189	7.7
190-199	7.0
200-204	6.5
205-209	5.9
210-214	5.0
215-219	3.9
220-224	3.2
225-229	2.9
230-239	2.1
240 and Over	0.4
Overall	5.7

books for shorter intervals, although going much below a year of exposure can be misleading. ★

A more general and considerably more useful report on delinquency by score is shown in the Appendix.

II.4.1.6 Dynamic Delinquency Reports.

An important report that can be produced for tracking a portfolio is the Dynamic Delinquency Report. This report displays the status of delinquency of groups of accounts that have been on the books for equal amounts of time. This allows management to compare accounts that have been on the books for, say, six months with accounts opened at earlier dates when these earlier accounts had been on the books for six months, and similarly for as many other time intervals as may be desired. The time that an account is on the books is known as the *exposure time*, since this is the amount of time that the account has been exposed to the possibility of becoming delinquent.

Figure 45 shows an example of a Dynamic Delinquency Report. The left hand column shows the quarter in which groups of accounts were opened. The remaining columns show what percentage of the accounts opened in each of the indicated quarters had become 30 days delinquent in each of those quarters.

Figure 45

Sample Dynamic Delinquency Reports Showing
Percent of Portfolio 30 Days Delinquent

Quarter Opened	- - - - - Quarter Reported - - - - -						
	Q-2	Q-3	Q-4	Q-5	Q-6	Q-7	Q-8
1	2.1	9.4	20.6	27.2	33.6	37.4	40.2
2		2.0	9.7	18.9	25.4	35.1	36.8
3			2.1	9.1	21.3	28.6	32.8
4				2.2	9.0	20.9	26.9
5					2.0	9.6	19.9
6						1.9	9.4
7							2.1

---

[1] The frequency of this report depends on the volume of business. If the volume is high this report could be produced monthly or even more often. In most cases the volume is such that a quarterly report is sufficient.

This figure and Figure 46 both show normal cases with no peculiarities. For example, the bold faced figures running diagonally across Figure 45 show that accounts that had been open for two quarters had a 30 day delinquency rate around 9.4% with no dramatic departures from that figure. Similarly, other diagonals show no great variation. Furthermore, each row shows about the same rate of increase. The level of delinquency of these accounts rises quite steeply in the early quarters and then levels off.

Note that these figures are for 30 day delinquency, which can be expected to be considerably higher than percentages of accounts in higher stages of delinquency. These figures, like all of those in this book, are illustrative and should not be taken as typical or desirable.

Figure 46 shows the same type of information, this time for accounts that have become 90 days delinquent. Note that in this case the first quarter reported is Quarter 4, not Quarter 2 as in Figure 45, since an account must be on the books at least 3 months before it can become 90 days delinquent. The delinquency percentages are lower in Figure 46, since fewer accounts reach this level. However, the diagonals are fairly steady and the rows show the same sorts of rates of increase.

Figure 46
Sample Dynamic Delinquency Report Showing
Percent of Portfolio 90 Days Delinquent

Quarter Opened	----- Quarter Reported -----						
	Q-4	Q-5	Q-6	Q-7	Q-8	Q-9	Q-10
1	0.2	1.2	2.8	3.6	4.8	5.3	5.8
2		0.2	1.1	2.8	3.2	4.9	5.2
3			0.1	1.4	3.0	3.7	4.8
4				0.2	1.5	2.7	3.5
5					0.2	1.2	2.9
6						0.3	1.1
7							0.2

Obviously, Dynamic Delinquency Reports can be produced showing the percentages of accounts in other stages of delinquency or they can show other data. For example, the table might show, instead of percentages of accounts delinquent, the total dollars delinquent or the actual count of accounts that are delinquent. They can also be produced for accounts with different scores. From time to time each user will decide for itself which of the various alternatives it prefers.

The normal cases shown in Figures 45 and 46 are very reassuring. Similar times on the books show similar and tolerable delinquencies, and delinquencies rise with exposure time and flatten out to an acceptable rate in a reasonable time. That is all very well, but what does the user do when the figures do not show these reassuring characteristics?

The first question a user should ask when an unexpected figure shows up on a Dynamic Delinquency Report is: Have we changed any of the conditions in our credit operation? Obviously, if the cut-off score is raised, the user should expect to find a decrease in the delinquency of those accounts accepted after the change, since the overall risk being taken is less, and the reverse will be true if the cut-off has been lowered. Similarly, if total dollars delinquent is shown in a table and the volume of business increases for any reason, an increase in the total dollars delinquent can be expected, even though the fraction of accounts delinquent may not change at all.

Figure 47 shows what might be expected of a report of 30 day delinquency (like Figure 45) if the cut-off score had been *lowered* at the beginning of Quarter 3. Note that from that row downward the fraction of accounts that are delinquent increases. This is known as a *row effect* since all rows after the time of the change in the cut-off show an increase in delinquency along the diagonals of equal exposure.

Figure 47

Sample Dynamic Delinquency Report Showing the Row Effect
of a Change in Cut-off Score in Quarter 3

Quarter Opened	- - - - - Quarter Reported - - - - -						
	Q-2	Q-3	Q-4	Q-5	Q-6	Q-7	Q-8
1	2.1	9.4	20.6	27.2	33.6	37.4	40.2
2		2.0	9.7	18.9	25.4	35.1	36.8
Cut-off score lowered beginning next quarter							
3			3.1	10.5	24.3	31.6	36.8
4				3.2	10.8	25.9	30.9
5					3.1	11.7	23.9
6						3.0	11.4
7							3.3

Another case is the so-called *column effect*. This shows up when some condition external to the user's credit operation affects the economy of the user's credit population. For example, if taxes were suddenly increased and the users of credit had less disposable cash, the dynamic delinquency report can be expected to show an increase in the fraction of the accounts that are in the early stages of delinquency starting in the quarter in which the tax increase took effect and continuing for some time after that event. Figure 48 shows what a column effect might look like if a tax increase reduced disposable income after Quarter 5. ★

Figure 48

Sample Dynamic Delinquency Report Showing the Column Effect of Reduction in Disposable Income on 30 Day Delinquency After Quarter 5

Quarter Opened	- - - - - Quarter Reported - - - - -						
	Q-2	Q-3	Q-4	Q-5	Q-6	Q-7	Q-8
1	2.1	9.4	20.6	27.2	35.6	42.4	45.2
2		2.0	9.7	18.9	30.4	40.1	41.8
3			2.1	9.1	26.3	33.6	37.8
4				2.2	14.0	25.9	31.9
5					7.0	14.6	24.9
6						6.9	14.4
7							7.1

When any unexpected set of figures shows up on a dynamic delinquency report, the user of the system must look for a possible explanation. An explanation may be hard to find, but management should try. It is useful to know if the unexpected delinquency figures are associated with some action on the part of the credit grantor or if they are associated with phenomena outside its control. The scoring system manufacturer can be of help in these cases, since it is in touch with many users and may have information that is applicable to a broad range of scoring system users.

II.4.1.7 Diary.

A report that every scoring system user should maintain is a carefully dated diary of the operation. This need not be in any particular format and can be a simple narrative. It should be started as soon as the organization undertakes to acquire a scoring system and should record every important event in the course of the development of the system in which the user takes part. It should, for example, identify the individuals assigned to the Liaison team and the area of expertise of each. It should certainly record every material decision that is made or conclusion that is drawn.

The definitions of Good and Bad accounts should be recorded as well as the reject rate in effect at the time the development sample was drawn and also the percentage of the total portfolio of accounts that are classified as Bad. The initial cut-off score should be recorded as well as any changes in it. Review rules and rules covering overrides as well as modifications of either of these should be noted. In addition, any material change in credit conditions, such as area of coverage or credit limit rules, should be included. The names of the decision making staff members should be included, along with the dates of their tenure.

II.4.2 Change of Cut-off Score.

A question frequently asked by new users of credit scoring systems is: "When should we change our cut-off score?" The user should be prepared to adjust the cut-off score very shortly after installation if it is shown that the reject rate is markedly different from that predicted by the statistics of the system. For example, the development data may show that a score of 200 points will reproduce the 40% rejection rate experienced before scoring was installed, and this number may be set as the initial cut-off. After a month or so, or whenever sufficient applications have been received and scored so that a reliable figure for the rejection rate can be determined, it may be found that the rejection rate is only 35% or has increased to 45%.

If the general distribution of scores is similar to that of the original sample with the exception that the whole set is shifted up or down, then a change in the cut-off will produce the desired rejection rate. It is rare that it is necessary to adjust the cut-off score by more than a few points, if at all.

Later on, after the scoring system has been in operation for a while and there has been sufficient time for changes in external conditions and in internal credit department policies and goals to take effect, it may be useful to examine the cut-off score. A user may decide to reduce his overall risk in which case he should raise the cut-off by the amount the basic statistics suggest. Alternatively, a user may decide to accept a higher risk and improve the way in which collections are carried out, in which event a lowering of the cut-off score would be appropriate.

From time to time a user will modify the cut-off score for a particular purpose. For example, a credit grantor may decide to try to attract some group not previously sought out as customers, such as students at some particular college or university, or a minority group that has not yet shown any particular interest in the offering of the user. In such a case the credit grantor may choose to use a cut-off score different from the usual one in order to buy into a particular market, being fully aware that there is a cost to such an action.

A credit grantor should *not* change his cut-off score as a reaction to change in external conditions, without careful thought. On more than one occasion in my experience credit grantors have considered changing their cut-off scores when the local economy suffered an unexpected reverse. In these cases management felt that it should "tighten up" by raising the cut-off, thus avoiding some losses.

There are two things wrong with this idea. First of all, a change in the cut-off, no matter how drastic, will only affect new applicants and will do nothing whatever to improve the quality of the accounts now on the books. Any change in cut-off score will not be reflected in a corresponding change in the quality of the overall customer population until accounts opened under the new cut-off form an appreciable fraction of the whole population, a condition that may take a long time to show up.

A second reason for caution in changing (especially raising) the cut-off in the face of an economic reverse is that it is not necessarily true that it will have any effect on the customer population. The impulse to raise the cut-off is based on a feeling that the risk measured by the scoring system will be altered by the changed economy. It is entirely possible that this could be the case, but there is no evidence to support it. When an economic downturn takes place, people do not rush out to open credit accounts that they suspect they will not be able to pay. Experience has shown that when an economic reverse takes place, the volume of applications drops as people exercise caution in extending themselves in the face of uncertainty.[1]

Even after the stock market crash of 1987 there was no particularly severe change in credit performance, although many people did indeed cut back on its use. What might happen in the event of a major

---

[1] It is also my experience that accounts already on the books show a temporary increase in short term delinquency that quickly diminishes as people figure out how to cope with the new conditions, along with a small increase, also usually temporary, in the rate of serious delinquency. By and large, however, people are very sensible about the use of credit and reduce its use when they is not confident about what will happen next.

disaster like a global war or a world wide depression like that of the 1930s is another matter. With a little luck we will never have to face the problem since neither I nor anyone else can give you good advice on the subject.

The cut-off score should never be changed as a cure for a suspected malfunction of the scoring system. No change in the cut-off will cure a failed scoring system, what is needed in such a case is an entirely new scoring system. This situation is discussed in the following section.

II.4.3 The Decision to Replace a Scoring System.

There are two reasons for replacing a scoring system. The first is that it can no longer distinguish Good from Bad accounts to the degree originally expected. The second is that the goals and practices of the credit grantor are undergoing change.

Scoring systems do not abruptly change their performance. The continued effective performance of a scoring system can be measured by the report of Delinquency by Score and Exposure. The Population Stability Report and the Characteristic Analysis Report can each foretell possible departures from expected performance when the population is changing.

When a scoring system shows that it is departing from expectation, the user must decide when to replace it. The dynamics of credit, with some influences under the control of the user and many entirely outside his control, make it difficult to predict with any precision when a system should be replaced.

Only rarely are credit scoring systems replaced due to failure to perform as expected. If the underlying population does not change and the general economy is steady, the life of a scoring system is quite long. I personally have no experience with a scoring system that has stopped performing when there has been no change in the credit environment in which it operates; they are remarkably robust. However, a degradation in performance due to any of a variety of circumstances is always possible, and managements must pay attention to the reports of system performance in case an unexpected or unexplained degradation does take place.

Credit managements are well advised to give thought in advance to the degree of degradation of the performance of their scoring system that would cause them to replace it. Since system performance degrades slowly, if at all, if internal policies have not changed, management can predict when the replacement should take place and can plan the assembly of the sample data that will be needed for the development of the new system.

Systems are usually replaced because the user has changed its manner of doing business in one way or another. One type of change that frequently takes place is the broadening of the market. The credit grantor decides to offer his products to a population to which it has not previously been offered. He may expand his geographical coverage or seek population segments in his normal geography he has not previously sought.

When a genuinely new population is to be added to a portfolio there is usually no information available about that new population on which to base a decision regarding scoring. One way to develop the needed information is to begin the expansion into the new population slowly, using the existing scoring system as a device to limit losses. Population Stability and Characteristic Analysis data can be produced and compared with similar data from the original population. If the populations are substantially the same and the details of the individual characteristics are reasonably similar, then the user has some grounds to be confident that the original scoring system will be sufficiently effective to begin business on a larger scale.

On the other hand, if the statistics show that the new population is markedly different from the original, management has a different problem altogether. If the enterprise has experience with the new population but had not applied scoring to it, then it has available the information it needs to develop a scoring system for that new population.

If there is no experience, then experience must be acquired. This can be done with appropriate caution by starting business with the new population using either their current scoring system or one invented specifically for start-up use. Most manufacturers have experience in start-up cases in which an invented scoring system is used so as to avoid serious losses during the time that information is being gathered for a tailored scoring system.

Another reason that can be advanced for the replacement of a scoring system is that the products to be offered are about to be changed. If an enterprise that has previously offered only automobile loans decides to stop doing automobile business and, instead, to issue a credit card, that organization has good grounds to believe that the populations seeking the new product will be different enough to merit a new scoring system. However, this is a most unlikely scenario; credit grantors may add a product but do not usually suddenly replace one. As a result, there may be grounds for developing a new scoring system to serve the population seeking the new product, but this does not call for the replacement of the original system if it is still serving the original population in an acceptable manner.

The steps to be taken when a credit grantor decides to add a product to its portfolio are similar to those taken when addressing a new population. A purely artificial scoring system can be used to limit losses while developing a sample of real cases that can be used as the basis for the production of a scoring system based on real data.

A credit grantor may consider replacing a scoring system if he makes a drastic change in credit policy. For example, if a creditor decided to increase his credit limits by a large factor, he might be concerned that the population that the new policy will attract will be very different from his original population. In such a case, the original system might lose some effectiveness.

Prudence suggests that the original scoring system be applied to the new population but that it be monitored carefully to detect differences from the original one. If none are detected, and if overall delinquency performance is unchanged, then the original scoring system can be applied with confidence. If changes are detected, the process is well under way to collect the data that will be needed for the development of a targeted scoring system.

II.4.4 Analysis and Experimentation.

Many of the comments made in the previous section on the replacement of scoring systems are in the nature of designs for experiments to be carried out and suggestions for analyses that can be made. When a new population is sought for a credit portfolio or when new products are to be offered to an existing or perhaps a new population, information must be gathered before a decision can be made as to the applicability of some existing scoring system or the need for a new one. It should be kept in mind that the gathering of information takes time and is accomplished at some cost.

An application scoring system permits some experiments to be undertaken that can improve its performance. There are two experiments that any application scoring system user should undertake. The first measures the cost of its policy on the use of credit bureau information and the second is to measure the cost of its policy on overrides.

As noted in Section II.3.3, the points to be assigned to credit bureau information are frequently added to the credit score after the points for the application information have been assigned. This is done on the grounds that if a decision can be made on application data alone, the expense of a credit bureau report can be avoided. While many users are quite willing to accept the decision of the scoring system on the low side (that is, if an applicant develops a score so low that no number of points obtained from a good credit report will put the application over the cut-off), they are usually unwilling to accept the decision of the scoring system on the high side, when the application score is so high that the most negative credit bureau points will not reduce the final score below the cut-off.

Many credit grantors prefer to pay the price and buy a credit report for any applicant who receives an acceptable score on application information alone, no matter how high, and will tend to reject an applicant with what they consider a poor credit report.

While this is not an unreasonable position where a scoring system is being installed where none has been in place before, it is expensive and merits examination. The experiment requires that some high scoring applicants who have poor credit reports be accepted and their performance evaluated. If it turns out that these applicants, accepted despite a poor credit bureau report, perform as the score predicts, then the purchase of the credit report is a waste of money. On the other hand, if they do not perform according to score, then an investigation should be made to see what changes should be made in the credit bureau points to bring the scoring system prediction into correspondence with account performance. H

The user can start such an experiment by working down from the top of the score scale. Start with a group of applications with very high scores but which have poor credit reports. Take such a group with scores representing odds much better than the odds at cut-off, say 16 times better (this means that if the cut-off odds are 10 to 1 to be Good, the group will show application scores corresponding to 160 to 1 or better, suggesting that they are very good risks). Accept some of these applications and see how they perform. If these accounts perform better than the cut-off odds, that is, better than 10 to 1, then the purchase of the credit bureau report was a waste of money since the account has proved that it could safely have been accepted without the report.

Once the group at 160 to 1 has proved its value without the credit bureau report, the user should try the same experiment on a group scoring somewhat less than this first group. Once again the performance of a small group of such accounts can be measured and a determination made as to whether or not the credit bureau report was worth the price. Substantial savings can be made as a result of this experiment.

Analysis of intuitional overrides can improve system performance. The analysis is straightforward: keep accurate records of the override decisions that accept applications that score under the cut-off, including the identity of the individual who made each one and the reason given in each case. Follow these accounts and see how they perform. If the odds at cut-off are, say, 10 to 1, and the accounts accepted below the cut-off perform at *less* than those odds, then the overrides are costing money.

Careful analysis of who makes which overrides may show that some analysts do it better than others, but my experience has been that the scoring system will beat the individual making an override if any substantial number of cases are involved. When it is made clear that overrides are reducing the profits of the organization, management has the ammunition it needs to end the practice.

A more difficult problem concerns the overrides that turn down applicants who score over the cut-off. There is, of course, no record of how these would have performed had they been accepted. An experiment here requires that the override be reversed, a procedure that can be difficult to establish. The idea is to take some of these overrides, so-called "high side overrides" and accept them, noting carefully that an override was recommended (and who made it) and then waiting to see what happens. Time must elapse before such accounts (as any others) mature enough to measure Good and Bad performance.

The results will determine the action that management should consider taking. If the accounts turn out to perform as the scoring system predicted, by far the most likely outcome, then the override was an unsound decision. Lost accounts cost the credit grantor dollars and goodwill, the avoidance of unwisely rejected accounts is to the benefit of the applicants and to the credit grantor.

Part III

Beyond Application Scoring

III.1 The Need For Further Scoring Systems.

When credit scoring was introduced in the United States nearly thirty years ago, consumer credit was almost entirely a matter of the granting of loans or extending credit for relatively short terms. People bought cars, washing machines, refrigerators and the like or borrowed money for periods from six months to three years. However, it was not long before the idea of revolving credit began to spread. In this form, a borrower had credit available to him for an indefinite period, most commonly in the form of a credit card.

Revolving credit had been pioneered by, among others, the petroleum companies. In the days before the unsolicited distribution of credit cards was prohibited by law, every college and university senior in the United States could expect to receive at least one oil company card, and frequently half a dozen, in the course of his final year at school. This type of credit, which might be termed "captive", provided the customer with a card that could be used only at the grantors' establishments. Major retailing chains like Sears, Wards, and Penneys were not far behind, followed quickly by the major department store chains.

Revolving credit that was not tied to a particular credit grantor, which might be termed "general" credit, was introduced by American Express and by the Bank of America through their BankAmericard® (which later became Visa). Once introduced, the bank cards exploded; Master Charge (later Master Card) came in as a challenge to Visa and almost every bank felt that it must issue one or the other or both.

In the initial stages, with every bank seeking customers, bank cards were issued without fee, and it was not uncommon for people to have ten or twenty such cards. Newspapers, on otherwise dull days, would photograph the wallets of individuals who had hundreds, and for all I know, thousands of cards. This proliferation did not last long; the banks began to charge for their cards and the number of cards per wallet dropped quickly to one or two.

Even before the bank cards became popular, users of scoring systems were asking how long they could rely on the estimation of risk represented by the score. Since it came to be understood that the risk presented by an individual borrower was not some permanent feature of his character, the length of time a score could be depended on became a subject of great interest. Every credit grantor had his own stories of individuals who came on the books, paid without flaw for a year or more and then suddenly went bad. How could problems of this sort be handled?

The answer was clear enough once the problem was recognized; build a scoring system based on purchase and payment behavior and use it on an on-going basis, updating the estimate of risk for each account regularly as time goes on. It certainly made sense to suppose that the behavior of a borrower in the future could be better predicted from his behavior as a borrower up to the present than from the information on an increasingly distant credit application. The past year's purchase and payment behavior should be a better predictor of next month's payment behavior than whether or not the borrower had a checking account some time in the past.

This supposition proved, on examination, to be well founded. The product now known as *Behavior Scoring* was born. Fair, Isaac and Company produced its first behavior scoring system for Montgomery Ward in the late 1960s.

The problems and opportunities presented by revolving credit were not limited to the collection of delinquent accounts, important as that is. In revolving credit many other decisions have to be made: decisions involving the setting and modification of credit limits, what to do with accounts that are over their limits, whether or not to re-issue a card when it expires, the authorization of purchases, and the marketing of products to the customer base. Decisions in each of these areas can be approached through the use of a behavior scoring system far more easily than could be done by trying to get the customer to fill in a new application every time a decision was to be made.

III.2 Behavior Scoring.

The mathematics of the development of a behavior scoring system is almost exactly the same as that used in the production of an application scoring system, but the way the data is prepared for use is considerably different.

As is the case with an application score table, what is needed here is a body of Good and Bad accounts. In this case, of course, the accounts to be used are among those already on the books. An examination of the current master file can identify a body of accounts satisfying a definition of Bad and another satisfying a definition of Good. As in the application case, the definitions of Good and Bad must be objective and such that a computer program can be written to identify them.

Once the selected Good and Bad accounts have been identified, the master file is searched for the data that was known about those accounts some months earlier. Each of the items of information on the master file that was known about the Good and Bad accounts at the earlier time is eligible for consideration as a candidate Characteristic. In addition, various combinations of those items can be constructed to form generated characteristics, also eligible for inclusion in any scoring system.

The purpose here is to determine from the data known at any given time, what the risk is that an individual will go bad at some later time. Unlike an application scoring system, the behavior scoring table can be applied to the accounts every month, as a part of the normal billing cycle during which each account is examined, so that any changes in the risk position of any given account can be detected.

The procedure outlined above sounds good enough but, since many credit grantors did not, in the early days, retain enough information in the billing system master file, it was frequently impossible to follow it. A more common practice was to start by designing a master file format that would contain the kind of information that would be needed.[1]

In many cases a creditor, knowing that he would get involved in behavior scoring sooner or later, set about getting the proper files well in advance, making the actual score table construction a great deal faster than would have been the case had he had to await the creation of the sample.

Once a master file is designed and in place, data begins to accumulate. When enough data are available, anywhere from six to eighteen

---

[1] The difficulties that developed in the early days usually stemmed from the fact that data processing installations put a premium on speed of processing, with the result that master files all too often contained only that information needed for the current billing cycle. Equipment now available has made these restrictions disappear.

months later, "time zero" is declared and the clock is started. Six months or so later, "observation time", it is possible to identify some accounts as Good and others as Bad. If there are enough of each, the scoring system can be constructed based on the data on the master file, already in machine usable form.

Various approaches are used in the construction of the sample on which the scoring system is to be based. One is to use the entire portfolio of accounts and to build the system on accounts that were Good at "time zero" but which were divided between Good and Bad at "observation time". Another is to use only that sub-set of the accounts on the books that had, at time zero, reached the first level of delinquency that is recognized by the creditor. In some cases that could be five days late, in others as much as thirty days late.

However the behavior scoring system is produced, the final result is a score table that can be implanted in the billing system of the user that will calculate, each time an account in the selected group is examined, the risk that it will become an unsatisfactory account in the near future.[1]

The use of behavior scoring leads to a curious paradox. Behavior score measures the risk presented by an account under whatever policies existed at the time the system was constructed. However, a behavior scoring system is installed for the express purpose of changing the previous policies depending on the behavior score achieved by each account. Once the behavior score is installed and an explicit strategy, based on behavior score, is designed for, say, collections, the purpose of the whole operation is to reduce delinquencies. This means that an action will be taken on accounts depending on their score with the intention of *reducing* the probability that these accounts will become delinquent, that is, behave as the score predicts.

If the new strategy is successful, then accounts with a behavior score indicating, say, 1 to 13 odds for becoming delinquent will show by their actual performance odds of, say, 1 to 18.★ Actual behavior will be better than that predicted by the scoring system. As a result, a user cannot measure the effectiveness of a behavior scoring system by comparing the actual risk demonstrated by accounts with the risk estimated originally by the behavior scoring system, since the whole

---

[1] By "selected group" I mean the population on which the behavior scoring table was developed. This might be the entire population of accounts or those that had reached some initial stage of delinquency or some other group considered suitable.

idea is to change the original risk estimate for the better. As a result of this paradox, the measure of the success of a behavior scoring system is not the accuracy of its measure of risk but the *relative* effectiveness of the new policies established by the management as compared with the results of earlier policies.

III.3 Behavior Scoring Practice.

As mentioned, behavior scoring is useful in a number of the decision areas of concern to a credit operation. It can be used either on its own or as a component in a more complex structure called "Adaptive Control", discussed in Section III.4.

III.3.1 Reissue.

Credit cards are usually valid for some fixed interval, frequently one year but often for two or three. Factors to be considered when deciding whether to reissue include the activity of the account, how long the account has been on the books, what sort of balances has the account shown, and, of course, the delinquency history, if any. A behavior score, when available, becomes an additional factor in reaching the reissue decision. Figure 49 shows a fairly simple kind of reissue strategy that can be employed when a behavior scoring system is in place.

Figure 49

Hypothetical Simple Reissue Strategy

Current Cycles Delinquent	Months Since Last Activity	Max. Cycles Ever Delinquent	Behavior Score	Reissue Card for Indicated Months
0	0 - 12	0 - 1	Below 320	18
			321 - 399	24
			400 or More	36
		2 or More	Below 320	12
			321 or More	18
	13 or More	n/a	n/a	0
1	0 - 12	0 - 1	Below 320	12
			321 or More	18
		2 or More	Below 320	0
			321 or More	12
	13 or More	n/a	n/a	0
2	n/a	n/a	n/a	0

n/a = not applicable

The strategy shown refers only to the current level of delinquency, along with a very coarse division of the activity on the account, the highest level of delinquency in the past, and the behavior score. Even with these simplified components, there are twelve separate alternatives. If additional factors are included, such as current account balance and time on books, the strategy can become quite complex. However, since these strategies are embedded in the computer program that examines all accounts each billing cycle, no appreciable burden is added to the processing time while a very considerable improvement in overall portfolio performance can be expected.

III.3.2   Credit Limit Modification.

Credit limit modification can have a striking effect on the overall performance of a credit operation. The higher the credit limits can be set without increasing the risk faced by the credit grantor, the more profitable the operation will be. A reasonable goal for a credit department is to provide each customer with a limit that will encourage him to use the credit and also remain a good risk.

At the time an account is accepted, a credit limit is assigned. This initial limit can either be a general one, under a strategy that grants the same amount of credit to all accepted accounts, or one that sets a different limit to different groups of applicants. The policy may consider various factors; the assets of the applicant, his liabilities, the type of employment, and any other items thought to be important.

Beginning as early as the first few months of the life of an account, the behavior of that account (and consequently the behavior score) may be such as to recommend that the credit limit be modified.

Management can construct a strategy table of the sort that is illustrated (in part) in Figure 50. This figure shows only the cases where the current delinquency is at most one cycle; the complete strategy would, of course, include the full range. Clearly, this strategy table can be made simpler or more complicated, depending on management's goals. It might be wise to start with a fairly simple strategy, measure its results, and then see if changes in it improve overall performance.

An action code rather than an action is given in the last column since the action to be taken in any one case may depend on several factors.

Figure 50

Portion of Hypothetical Credit Limit Strategy

Current Cycles Delinquent	Max Cycles Ever Delinq.	Months Since Last Activity	Months on Books	Behavior Score	Action Code
0	0	0 - 5	1 - 12	<128	0
				128 - 200	1
				201+	2
			13 or More	<128	0
				128+	2
		6 or More	n/a	n/a	0
	1 - 2	0 - 5	n/a	<200	0
				200+	1
		6 or More	n/a	n/a	0
	3+	n/a	n/a	n/a	0
1	0	0 - 5	1 - 12	<128	0
				128+	1
			13+	<128	0
				128+	1

Different credit limit modifications might be made depending on the current balance of the account, the fraction of the current limit that has been used, the highest fraction of the limit that has ever been used, and the time since the last change. As in the case of the reissue strategy, this strategy can be quite complex. As before, it might be well to begin with a fairly simple strategy until the manner of handling strategies is well understood.

Accounts should be considered for an increase in limit on a periodic basis, perhaps once a quarter or once every six months. It must also be possible to consider a credit limit increase when a customer asks for one. As in all cases of strategy tables, management should consider carefully what goal is being sought and make a table that best pursues that goal. The measurement of the performance of the strategy can be compared with that of any alternative strategy that may be tried.

III.3.3 Collections.

Collections is usually the first area of interest to every credit department considering the use of behavior scoring. In this area management can state the collection action that is to be taken at various levels of risk and, perhaps, at various levels of dollar delinquency. Figure 51 is a hypothetical example of what a collections strategy might look like for accounts that are 30 days past due. All sorts of alternatives are possible, and each credit operation will have special conditions that it will want to include.

Figure 51
Hypothetical Collections Policy on
Accounts 30 Days Past Due

Score	Dollars Delinquent			
	<$100	$100-$300	$301-$500	Over $500
Below 200	Letter #1	Phone Call	Phone Call	Atty. Letter
201 - 210	Letter #2	Letter #2	Phone Call	Phone Call
211 - 240	Statement Overprint	Letter #2	Letter #3	Phone Call
Over 240	Statement Overprint	Statement Overprint	Letter #2	Letter #3

Similar strategy tables will be needed for every other level of delinquency, and all must include consideration of all the factors that management feels should be included in the decision process.

Whenever a strategy of this sort is installed, it makes sense to provide space in the master file in which to record any action that is taken and when it took place, so that a later analysis can be made to examine the effectiveness of each possible action.

In what fraction of the cases did the statement overprint result in payments that made up the delinquent amounts? Were the various letters effective? Do the phone calls produce results? The answers to these questions can lead to modifications to some parts of the policy as well as to confirmation that other parts of the current policy are satisfactory.

III.3.4 Over Limit Accounts.

Despite the setting of credit limits, some accounts manage to exceed that limit. This can happen either as a result of a purchase authorization or as an accumulation of small purchases, each under the amount requiring authorization but which, when accumulated, go over the limit. In both cases a credit grantor should have a strategy on what should be done. Since the behavior score provides a measure of the risk presented by the account, management can establish a risk driven strategy that determines the action to be taken. As in the case of collections, credit grantors may wish to use a combination of behavior score and dollars over limit to determine the strategy, but some may have other criteria they wish to use in addition to or instead of the dollars over limit.

III.3.5 Authorization.

The technology of authorization is improving rapidly. In the past it was quite difficult to control authorizations, particularly over long distances and multiple time zones. For example, it was hard for a Californian traveling in Asia to get speedy authorization for almost any purchase. If credit grantors allowed purchases to be made without authorization for large amounts, their exposure to fraud and other losses was serious.

Nowadays communications are becoming faster and more convenient so that it is much easier to provide authorizations. However, even though communications are quicker and cheaper, there is an enormous volume of demand for authorizations, and speed of response is more and more important; the buying customer does not like to be kept waiting and the seller does not want to lose a sale.

Behavior scoring provides credit management with a useful tool around which to build an authorization strategy. Such a strategy would consider not only behavior score, but current delinquency, if any, previous delinquency, current credit limit and the relation between the current balance and the limit, as well as any authorization history that may be available. It is also wise to consider whether or not the proposed purchase, if authorized, will bring the balance over the limit.

Improvements in technology will be of considerable help in improving authorizations. Authorizations of purchases in the cases of captive credit cards are relatively easy, since each point of sale is connected directly to the central billing system and the authorization program can be invoked at the time the sale is rung up. Delays in such cases are usually brief, since many authorizations can be made automatically according to a strategy table embedded in the enterprise's computer and delays only occur when the program decides that human intervention is required.

Authorization of purchases in general credit, where the card is not tied to a particular retailing chain, are considerably more difficult. The customer may be in one location and the credit grantor a half a world away. In these cases communication has to be established with some point that can make a decision. Technological improvements in communications are making this easier all the time.

Further improvements in card technology, especially those permitting the card to carry magnetically coded information that can be interrogated and modified by the point of sale device, will make many of the authorization calls unnecessary. If the card shows that there is ample space under the credit limit for the contemplated purchase, the credit grantor may establish a strategy that no call is required and the purchase can be approved automatically.

Alternatively, if the purchase is for an amount over some figure set by the credit grantor, then a call must be made to some intermediate point where a behavior score can be calculated and a strategy applied.

Only the rare cases that cannot be settled at the point of sale or by an intermediate decision point will be sent all the way back to the credit grantor for a final resolution. As it becomes possible to deliver copies of full master files to intermediate decision points, it will become possible to make nearly all decisions either locally or at these intermediate points, without having to have recourse to the central file.

III.3.6 Solicitation for Marketing.

Many credit grantors are involved in marketing various products to their customer base. Frequently, this is done by inserting stuffers in the billing material in the hope that the customer will buy the offered merchandise at the time he pays his bill. In other cases the merchandising material is sent separately.

Whatever the means that are used to deliver the marketing material to the customer, it is an expensive process. It is particularly expensive when it is sent to a customer who will not respond to it or, worse, will respond by ordering but then failing to pay. If the mailing is to be sent only to some part of the customer base, it makes sense to consider the behavior score of those customers and to send solicitation material only to those most likely to pay for materials ordered.

III.4 Adaptive Control.

While behavior scoring is a powerful tool all by itself, it is made even more powerful when it is a component of a system that can examine alternative credit control strategies and can adapt to changing conditions. Such a system can continually seek the best set of strategies.

Every credit department operates under management policies. In many cases these policies are unwritten and are passed on, sometimes with unintended modifications, from one supervisor to his successor. Many policies are written, although they are frequently more exhortatory than practical.

Credit scoring, both for applications and for behavior, can be a key component in the objective declaration of credit policy. Once a policy has been stated in objective terms, a computer can be used to implement all those facets of the policy that do not require human participation.

For the purpose of this discussion, I will refer to policies specified in sufficient detail that they can be installed in a computer, in whole or in part, as I have in previous sections, as strategies.

As soon as a strategy has been specified, it is appropriate to ask the question: "Is this the best strategy for this particular purpose?" Answering this question with traditional operating techniques is difficult, if not impossible. In normal operations it is extremely difficult to apply two competing strategies to find out which is the better.

A product called Adaptive Control has been developed that makes possible the evaluation of alternative credit strategies. An adaptive control system is a mixture of software and human participation which allows two (or more) credit strategies in any particular credit decision area to be operated at the same time, and for the performances of each to be measured so that their performances can be compared. Furthermore, it is specifically designed so that once the package of software is in place, new strategies can be installed and old ones removed or modified without having to call for the participation of the organization's data processing facility.

Figure 52 shows schematically the flow of events that takes place when an adaptive control system is *not* in operation and a single strategy is being applied. The example shown is the case of collections. The performance goals are provided to the Collections Manager by the executives to whom he reports. These goals are frequently set in terms of an operating budget and personnel allowance, along with some statement as to the fraction of the dollars that should be collected from the accounts in the various stages of delinquency.

Figure 52
Flow Diagram of Conventional Collections Operation

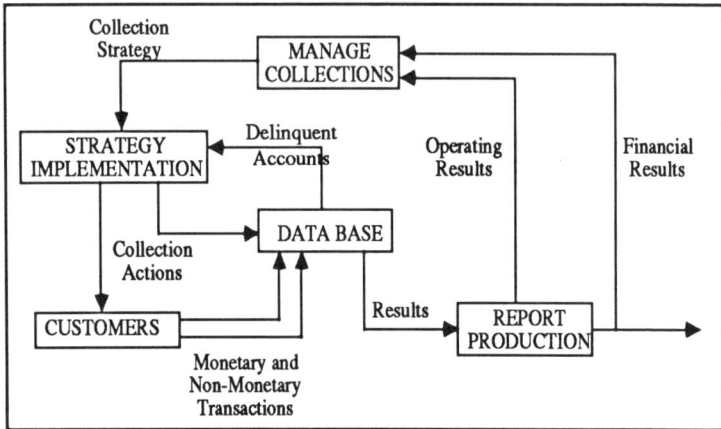

The Collections Manager translates the performance goals he is given into a collection strategy which relates the conditions of delinquent accounts (their degree of delinquency, their outstanding balances, previous delinquent history, and any other facts known about them) to various actions that the collections department can take.

Possible actions include (in addition to doing nothing) statement overprints, collection letters, phone calls, visits, legal action, charge off, and the sale of the account to a collection agency.

The flow of events starts with the customers themselves. The customer data base receives information from and about the customers in the form of purchase vouchers, payments, and non-monetary transactions such as address changes, requests for limit changes, responses to telephone calls, and so on. The data base provides the information needed to prepare customer bills as well as the data from which reports are prepared.

Broadly speaking, reports are in two categories, financial and operational. Financial reports in collections show, in various forms, the amounts delinquent at various intervals and the amounts collected. These reports are sent to other departments of the enterprise as well as back to the Collections Manager. Operational results report the various actions taken on different groups of accounts.

The data base is the source of information to the collections department regarding the delinquent accounts. The organization's collection strategy is applied to each of the delinquent accounts and the appropriate action is specified for each one. The specified action is then taken, either automatically (if the action called for is a statement overprint or a collection letter) or the necessary instructions are delivered to a member of the collections staff. Information about these actions is added to the customer data base so that reports can be produced.

The general flow of information in the case of an adaptive control system is similar to that shown in the figure, except that the interior of the box marked "Strategy Implementation" is very different. In the case where an adaptive control system is not in operation, the contents of the Strategy Implementation box consist of a table that associates account conditions with collection actions.

All of the delinquent accounts in some particular condition will be treated in exactly the same way. The table may be of some complexity, dividing the delinquent accounts into numerous categories, but all the members of any category will receive the same treatment.

When an adaptive control system is in place, the Strategy Implementation box is considerably more complex, as is shown in Figure 53.

Figure 53

Components of Strategy Implementation In An
Adaptive Control System

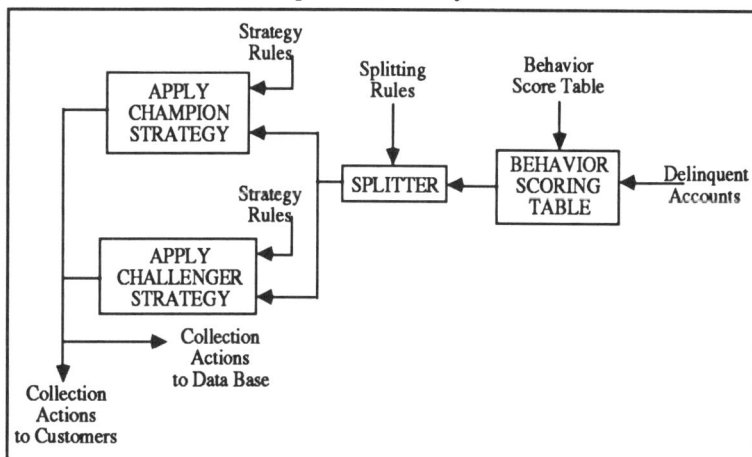

The inputs and outputs of the overall box are essentially the same as in the previous figure. The inputs consist of the data on each delinquent account, the rules governing each of the strategies, as well as the rules that determine which accounts go to which strategy. The outputs are the collection actions to be taken in each case and the information about these actions that is sent to the data base.

In the case of Adaptive Control, the Strategy Implementation box contains the the following components:

1. A behavior scoring table, that may or may not be present in the operation illustrated by the Figure 52.

2. At least two strategies. The number of strategies that can be tested at any one time depends on the volume of accounts that is available. If the portfolio is small and the total number of delinquent accounts is correspondingly low, two strategies may be all that can be tested at one time, since if more are tested there will be so few accounts in any one of the strategies that it will take an inordinately long time for results to develop.

   If the portfolio is very large and the number of delinquents is high, then it may be possible to tests a number of strategies.

   Normally, the procedure is to compare the strategy currently considered the best with one or more proposed alternative strategies. It has become customary to call the current strategy the "Champion" and all proposed alternatives "Challengers". The result of the test will determine whether the Champion will retain its title or be replaced by one of the Challengers, in which case the successful Challenger becomes the new Champion, and the old Champion is either discarded or reduced to the status of Challenger.

   As in the single strategy case, the rules that define each of the strategies are provided by the Collections Manager in response to goals set by senior management.

3. A box marked "Splitter". This is the point at which a decision is made to send a particular account to one or another of the strategies under examination. It is essential that the overall body of accounts sent to each of the contending strategies be what can be

called "statistically identical". This means that their overall behavior score distributions must be the same and the statistics of the degrees and amounts of delinquencies must be the same. This is a difficult problem and received a great deal of attention in the course of the design of the software. Clearly, if only high delinquencies go to one strategy and low ones to another, the results will not permit any general conclusions to be drawn.

While the overall flow of information in the case of an adaptive control system is similar to that of a single strategy process, a separate figure will help to identify the differences in the two cases. Figure 54 is similar to Figure 52, but there are some material differences. The Strategy Implementation box now has the capacity to handle several strategies. Management must also provide the splitting rules that determine what fraction of the accounts go to each strategy. Management will also provide the behavior scoring table.

Figure 54

Flow diagram of Adaptive Control System

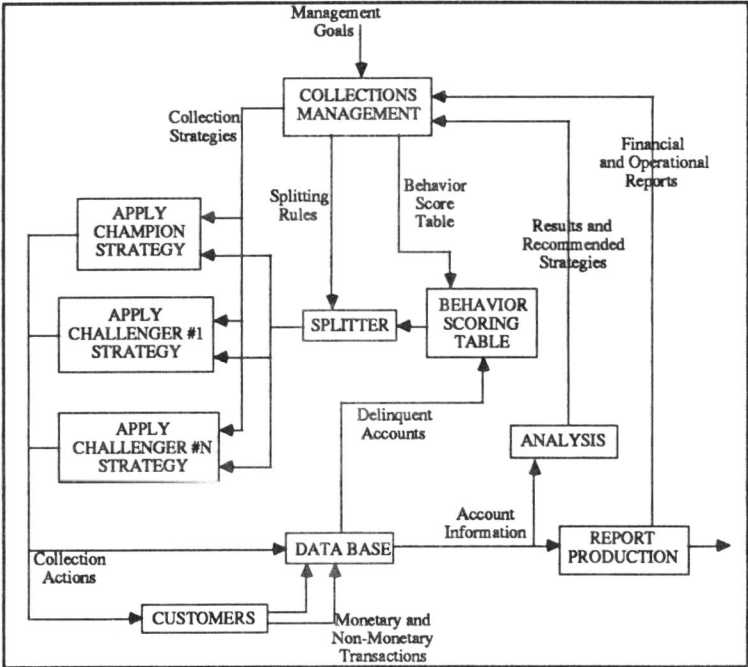

A change of equal importance is the new box labeled "Analysis". This is the place in the process that calls for the most important human participation. As in Figure 52, reports are produced regarding the financial and operational results of the overall collections operation. The new box, however, is the point in the process where the results produced by the competing strategies are compared and conclusions drawn as to which is better.

In addition, this place in the information flow is where proposed new Challenger strategies are developed and are recommended to management. As always, the final decisions as to the choice of Champion and the nature of the Challengers remain with management.

A major decision for credit management (or perhaps the management senior to it) is: How large a fraction of the accounts are to be sent to the Challenger (or Challengers)? This is a critical decision, since if too few go to the Challengers it will take a long time for the results to accumulate in sufficient volume to permit conclusions to be drawn. At the other extreme, if too many accounts go to Challengers, and those Challengers are drastic departures from the practice embodied in the current Champion, there is a risk that the results will be dangerous to the enterprise.

Note that the Champion/Challenger contest is not a one-time event. Conditions are constantly changing and the goals of the enterprise itself are subject to modification from time to time, so it is necessary to continue to challenge whatever Champion is in place; it is always possible that an improvement can be made.

For an adaptive control system to have real practical value within the user organization, credit management must be able to replace strategies, modify the splitting rules, and replace the behavior scoring table without having to get on the queue of the company's data processing facility. A principal feature of the software of a well designed adaptive control system is that once it is installed in the general data processing facility, changes are made by credit management whenever it chooses to do so.

The initial software installation does, of course, require the cooperation of the data processing staff. Any changes that are made by credit management after installation have no impact on any other part of the data processing facility, nor do they adversely affect the timeliness of any part of the facility. What the software provides can be imagined as a large bank of control knobs that credit management can twist over a very wide range of settings. For example, it can cause the "splitter" to send any fraction of accounts it chooses to any of the competing strategies. It can set the percentage of accounts to be sent to a risky strategy at a low figure, 1 or 2%, until it can assure itself that the risk is not dangerous to the company. At that time management can increase the flow of accounts to the new strategy to as high a percentage as it chooses.

If a strategy is declared unsatisfactory, the fraction of accounts it receives can be set to zero, while a newly declared Champion may be sent 100% of the accounts until such a time as a new Challenger can be designed and installed.

Since strategies are represented by tables that associate account conditions with collection actions, the replacement of one strategy with another is a matter of replacing the elements of a table to be removed with the elements of the table that is to replace it. In a similar way, the "splitting" rules consist of a table that associates a percentage of the accounts with a strategy, and management may change these percentages at any time to any value from 0% to 100%.

The facility inside the "splitter" that ensures the statistical identity of the bodies of accounts sent to the various strategies is not changed when strategies or splitting rules are modified. The requirement for statistically similar bodies of accounts to go to each strategy remains in place no matter how many strategies there are or how the flow of accounts may be divided among the contenders.

The example chosen to illustrate the concept of Adaptive Control was collections strategy, but the same overall flow applies to the other credit decision areas as well. Adaptive control applies equally well to the strategy for handling over-limit accounts, the adjustment of credit limits, the decision to reissue a credit card, and the strategy for authorization. Once the basic software for adaptive control is in place it can be used in all areas of interest.

III.5 Conclusion.

Consumer credit in 1990 is a very different social process from the one that carried that title forty years ago. Tens of millions of people in what is called the Western World have become users of consumer credit, people who might have been denied it under traditional methods or who would not have considered applying for it under the conditions that obtained in 1950.

The sheer volume of credit operations, the demand by the public for access to consumer credit, and the rapid growth of a consuming society made it necessary to develop tools capable of managing a completely new financial phenomenon. Credit scoring was one of those new tools. The arrival of high volume data processing equipment in the years following the end of the Second World War made its development and its implementation possible.

The use of statistics to construct tools for the estimation of risk has now been with us for more than thirty years. Basic application scoring is a standard procedure almost anywhere that credit is granted on a large scale. Behavior scoring has been in place for nearly twenty years and its use is spreading rapidly.

There are now many people in the field of consumer credit who have never worked without a scoring system, in sharp contrast to the situation only a few years ago when most senior credit executives had reached their positions using traditional methods and were suspicious of any mathematical tool that contended that it was superior to the judgment of experienced people.

What next? Some of the extensions of credit scoring that are coming along are already sufficiently well developed that no great vision is needed to foretell their arrival. One that is already in place and providing notable service is the application of scoring to marketing.[1] Here scoring is used to screen mailing lists to select those customers most likely to respond to a solicitation for the sale of merchandise and to pay for it if it is ordered.

The mailing lists involved are usually those developed by credit reporting agencies, but this is not a requirement. What is needed is a body of information about the addressees that can be used as candidate characteristics in a scoring system.

The scoring system for screening mailing lists can be constructed in various ways, one of which is to develop a scoring table based on credit information (whether bureau information or from some other source) that estimates the likelihood of response. The enterprise planning the solicitation mailing can then specify the minimum level

---

[1] This is called "PreScore®" by Fair, Isaac and Co.

of likelihood of response that it considers appropriate, and all members of the mailing list with a score corresponding to a lower likelihood are removed from the list. There may be cases where high scorers are also eliminated. For example, if the solicitation is designed to encourage application for a credit card, individuals with very high scores may be considered "too good" in the sense that they probably already have all the credit cards they want and, consequently, a mailing to them would be a waste of resources.

As in the case of the adaptive control system, the concepts of experimentation and quantitative analysis are central to solicitation mailing. It is useful to set two strategies (and possibly more, if the volume is sufficient) and to test the effect on the overall results of various cutoff scores. Since some enterprises use mail solicitations as a regular component of their business, an effective mailing list screening process can result in a very high return on the investment.

Another application of scoring that can be expected to be available before very long are scoring systems that are developed for the use of small enterprises that do not have portfolios large enough to use to construct a scoring system of their own, such as small banks. There are large numbers of small banks that might like to use scoring but do not have enough accounts for a system tailored to their individual experience. However, it appears reasonable to pool the experience of a group of banks into a body of information that is large enough to permit the construction of a scoring system.

Clearly, such systems are not tailored exclusively to each of the banks in the pool, but if care is taken in the selection of the members of the pool, it is possible to construct a valid and powerful scoring tool.

A further application of scoring well along in development is the practice of including a score along with a credit bureau report. In this application the scoring system is used by a credit bureau to respond to a request for a report by sending not only the standard report but also a score. This score is indicative of the risk presented by the individual on whom the report is made, based on the information available to the credit bureau.

Credit bureau scoring can either be used by itself or as a contributor to a more comprehensive scoring procedure that combines information available to the credit grantor with that from the credit bureau.

It can be stated with some confidence that statistical scoring procedures will continue to grow throughout the field of consumer credit. It will face an interesting challenge in countries outside the Western World as these countries gradually become able to produce consumer products at a rate that permits purchase on credit rather than for cash.

Some of the countries in Eastern Europe are already accepting some credit cards, though frequently only from foreigners. However, pressure will slowly develop for the internal use of credit cards. This poses a most interesting problem — there is no credit experience on which to base any sort of scoring system. This is a challenge, not a bar.

What I think would be a reasonable course would be to introduce consumer credit as part of a series of experiments that would include the adaptation of scoring ideas from the West in carefully controlled cases. The hypothesis being tested would be: The use of the adapted credit scoring table on the population selected for the introduction of consumer credit will be superior to a non-statistical credit evaluation procedure with which it is to be compared.

The first experiments will, doubtless, be costly, since neither the grantors of credit nor its users have any real understanding of the role of consumer credit in society. They will have to learn by experience as has the rest of the world. If the experiments are carefully constructed and adequately managed, the introduction of consumer credit can be expected to be smooth and rapid.

The development of consumer credit on a wide scale in the Soviet Union and in China would be an enormous stimulant to the economy of the whole world. How it would affect the world's social structure is impossible to foretell, but it will be fascinating to watch.

Credit is not the only arena in which scoring can be applied. Scoring techniques have been applied to the selection of tax returns for auditing, for the selection of prison inmates for work release programs, and for the selection of personnel for various jobs.

The use of scoring in the tax area is of some interest, but it is not what could be called a growing field. The use of scoring techniques applied to personnel selection, however, appears to me to have broad applicability.

In any area where risk is a factor, scoring may be applied. The largest such area is Insurance. The whole concept of insurance involves the estimation of the likelihood that some event will happen. Risk estimation in insurance is of two types, one is applied to singular events (such as the likelihood of the collapse of a public stadium) and the other is applied to events of high frequency (such as the likelihood of an automobile accident).

Scoring does not seem to have much applicability to singular events, since scoring systems are developed through the analysis of large quantities of data. However, in the personal lines, where enormous amounts of information are available, scoring has a very definite place. Work is being done in this area, and it will be interesting to see how long it takes for underwriters to recognize the value of scoring.

The future never turns out exactly as we expect, but I am confident that scoring will grow and prosper. Scoring, even in the limited area of credit, has benefitted millions of people and will benefit millions more in the future. From a personal point of view, it has provided me with a career in which I take no little pride. I have had the privilege of working with a remarkably large number of fine people from whom I have learned a great deal. From my privileged position of retirement, I will continue to watch the development of scoring with undiminished interest.

APPENDIX

This Appendix goes into the problem of measuring the performance of a scoring system a little more deeply than was done in the main part of the text. This is because measurement of performance requires some mathematical computation that I have tried to keep out of the main text but which is unavoidable if the user wants to make some measurements himself rather than contract with the manufacturer or some other outside supplier for that service.

The three subjects covered are Delinquency by Score reports, Population Stability reports, and Characteristic Analysis reports.

Delinquency by Score.

The basic assertion made by a credit scoring system is that high scores are associated with high odds to be Good while low scores are associated with low odds to be Good. The relationship was shown in Figures 43 and 44 in Section II.4.1.5.

If it can be shown by a table such as Figure 43 or 44 that the delinquency rate goes down as score goes up, the scoring system is formally valid; it is possible to distinguish between Good and Bad accounts to some degree. However, it is also important to know how the current ability to distinguish between Good and Bad accounts compares with that ability at the time the scoring system was developed.

This comparison can be made by producing two tables. The first is the table that shows the number of Good and Bad accounts from the development sample in each of a dozen or so score intervals, from the lowest to the highest. Such a table, as shown in Figure 55, displays what the performance of the scoring system would have been had it been in place during the development period at the time of its delivery.

The second table to be produced is similar to the first but shows the number of scored Good and Bad accounts currently in the portfolio that came on the books 12 months ago. The easiest way to produce this table is to write a program that uses the main billing file as input. Figure 56 shows the sort of output such a program could produce. Note that in this case all of the counts below 200 points (the cut-off score in this hypothetical example) are lumped together, since they are overrides and relatively few. Note also that these overrides perform poorly, just as their scores would indicate. Figure 56 in-

Figure 55

Hypothetical Example of Counts
of Development Sample by Score

Score	Number of Goods	Number of Bads	Percent Bad
Below 170	1386	281	17%
170 - 179	760	70	8.0
180 - 189	851	63	6.8
190 - 199	940	48	4.9
200 - 209	905	39	4.1
210 - 219	920	25	2.6
220 - 229	931	17	1.8
230 - 239	857	12	1.4
240 - 249	770	7	1.0
250 - 259	586	5	0.8
260 - 289	433	1	0.2
289 and Over	111	1	0.9

Figure 56

Hypothetical Example of Counts of Accepted
Applicants on the Books for 12 Months

Score	Number of Goods	Number of Bads	% Bad Current	% Bad Devel.
Below 200	106	11	10.3	11.6
200 - 209	2690	115	4.1	4.1
210 - 219	2787	81	2.8	2.6
220 - 229	2714	42	1.5	1.8
230 - 239	2571	36	1.4	1.4
240 - 249	2295	26	1.1	1.0
250 - 259	1768	17	0.9	0.8
260 - 279	1291	4	0.3	0.2
280 and Up	320	2	0.6	0.9

cludes in the right hand column the Percent Bads from Figure 55 for comparison. In this case the two sets of figures for Percent Bads match very closely, demonstrating the continued efficacy of the scoring system.[1]

A more interesting table can be obtained by displaying not only the Bad accounts (according to the definition of Bad used in the development of the scoring system) but also showing accounts of lesser degrees of delinquency. In a revolving charge portfolio such as a general credit card it is also useful to show the number of accounts that were accepted and the number of these that activated. This type of table gives a more comprehensive picture of the state of the portfolio than do those concerning only Bad accounts. Figure 57 is a hypothetical example of such a table. Delinquency by Score tables should not be restricted to accounts on the books for 12 months. Other exposure times, both shorter and longer, are also of interest.

Figure 57

Hypothetical Example of Delinquency by Score Report
Including Bads and 30 and 60 Day Delinquencies
-- Exposure Time 12 Months --

Score	Accept	Active	Ever 30+ Days		Ever 60+ Days		Current Bads		Develop. Bads
			#	%	#	%	#	%	%
<200	120	117	84	72	55	47	11	10.3	11.6
200 - 209	2897	2805	1627	58	617	22	115	4.1	4.1
210 - 219	2942	2868	1606	56	545	19	81	2.8	2.6
220 - 229	2888	2756	1378	50	386	14	42	1.5	1.8
230 - 239	2810	2607	1251	48	261	10	36	1.4	1.4
240 -249	2574	2321	928	40	186	8	26	1.1	1.0
250 - 259	2402	1785	660	37	89	5	17	0.9	0.8
260 - 279	1944	1295	414	32	52	4	4	0.3	0.2
280 +	812	322	93	29	13	4	2	0.6	0.9

---

[1] The cell counts are larger for the Current Goods and the Current Bads since these are counts of the actual portfolio while the development sample was scaled to a total of 10,000 applicants.

Population Stability Report.[1]

Examination of the performance of a scoring system necessarily means looking at accounts that have been on the books long enough to have had time to show Good or Bad performance. It is also important to make sure that the population of current applicants is similar to the population on which the scoring system was developed, since that similarity is reasonable grounds for expecting the system to perform satisfactorily. If unexpected differences appear, the user has early warning of possible future problems.

An effective comparison of the current application population and the population on which the scoring system was constructed can be made by comparing the distribution of current applicant scores with those in the development statistics. The degree of similarity between the two distributions can be determined by calculating the Population Stability Index according to the following formula:[2]

$$\text{Population Stability Index} = \sum_{i=1}^{n}\left[\left(\frac{c_i}{C} - \frac{d_i}{D}\right) \times \left(\ln\left\{\frac{c_i}{C} \div \frac{d_i}{D}\right\}\right)\right]$$

where c_i is the count of current applicants in the i-th of a total of n intervals, C is the total count of current applicants, d_i is the count of members in the development sample in the i-th interval, and D is the total count of the development sample. In the formula, "ln" indicates the natural logarithm.

Figure 58 gives an example of the calculation of the Population Stability Index in a hypothetical case.

This Index measures the separation of the two distributions of scores. If the distributions represent Good and Bad accounts, as they do when the scoring system is being developed, it is desirable to have a large Index (or more properly, in the case of system development, Divergence), indicating a strong ability to differentiate between the two groups of accounts. In measuring the Population Stability of two applicant populations, on the other hand, what is sought is the smallest possible Index, indicating that the population is stable and that there has been little or no change in the flow of applicants.

---

[1] This subject was introduced in Section II.4.1.2.

[2] In the statistical literature this number is called the Divergence, a term introduced by Solomon Kullback in his book *Information Theory and Statistics*, most recently published by Peter Smith, Gloucester, Mass, in 1978.

Figure 58

Hypothetical Example of the Calculation of Population Stability Index

Appl. Score Interval	Development Number of Apps. d_i	$\dfrac{d_i}{D}$	Current Number of Apps. c_i	$\dfrac{c_i}{C}$	A $\dfrac{c_i}{C} - \dfrac{d_i}{D}$	$\dfrac{c_i}{C} \div \dfrac{d_i}{D}$	B $\ln\left(\dfrac{c_i}{C} \div \dfrac{d_i}{D}\right)$	$A \times B$
<160	1100	.110	587	.090	-0.020	.818	-0.201	.004
160 - 179	1200	.120	653	.100	-0.020	.833	-0.182	.004
180 - 189	700	.070	424	.065	-0.005	.929	-0.074	.000
190 - 199	800	.080	542	.083	0.003	1.038	0.037	.000
200 - 209	900	.090	613	.094	0.004	1.044	0.043	.000
210 - 219	950	.095	587	.090	-0.005	0.947	-0.054	.000
220 - 229	1000	.100	979	.150	0.050	1.500	0.405	.020
230 - 249	1500	.150	1241	.190	0.040	1.267	0.236	.009
250 +	1850	.185	901	.138	-0.047	0.746	-0.293	.014
TOTAL	10000		6527				**Stability Index**	**.051**

There are no fixed rules that define when a Population Stability Index is announcing trouble, but in general a value under 0.100 is felt to indicate that the current population is similar to the original and no action is called for. A value between 0.100 and 0.250 suggests that some investigation (such as an analysis of the characteristics, as will be discussed below) should be undertaken to look for the source of the difference.

A value over 0.250 suggests that some fairly substantial change has taken place either in the incoming population or in the policies of the user. For example, if the user invades some population group never before solicited, or if there is a substantial change in the national economy or there is changed activity by competitors, a change in the nature of the overall pattern of applicants can be expected.

Characteristic Analysis Report.

From time to time it is instructive to compare the individual characteristics of the current flow of applicants with those of the original development population. This is certainly called for if the Population Stability Index goes over 0.100, but even if it is below that level a periodic examination can warn of gradual changes in the population.

Characteristic Analysis compares, for each Characteristic, the Attribute counts in the original development population with those in the current applicant population.[1] Figure 59 shows the data for the analy-

---

[1] This subject was introduced in Section II.4.1.4.

sis of the Characteristic *Occupation*. Two columns show the percent of each population in each attribute, copying Figure 43. The next column shows the difference in these percentages, followed by a column showing the number of points for each of the attributes, taken from Figure 31. The last column is the product of the difference in percentage and the attribute points. The total of these products is -590, or -5.9 when we convert percentage to parts per hundred.

Figure 59

Hypothetical Example of Characteristic Analysis

	Percent in Development Sample	Percent in Current Population	Difference	Points	Product of Difference Times Points
Retired	10	10	0	45	0
Professional	20	10	-10	40	-400
Clerical	35	10	-25	31	-775
Sales	15	20	+5	22	110
Service	10	30	+20	16	320
All Other	5	15	+10	31	310
Blank	5	5	0	24	0

TOTAL	- 435

The final figure means that we can expect the average score of the current applicant population to be 5.9 points lower than the average score of the development population, based on the change in this characteristic alone. Changes in the other scored Characteristics can make the total of all the changes greater or less than this figure, so that attention should be given to each Characteristic separately as well as to the total change.

Performance Evaluation.

Each of the different tests for system performance has deficiencies. Although Delinquency by Score is probably the best measure of the performance of a scoring system, it cannot be prepared until the delinquencies appear, by which time considerable damage may have been done. The Population Stability Index can be misleading unless a careful analysis of the individual Characteristics is undertaken. Even Characteristic Analysis, while it will identify the source of score differences, will not tell a user what he should do about it.

Despite the deficiencies of the various tests, as a group they are effective in warning of coming difficulties or identifying present ones. Happily, the world does not offer abrupt changes except in the most unusual circumstances, situations that are impossible not to notice, so that changes in populations proceed sufficiently slowly that thought can be devoted to deciding how to accommodate to the changes. Scoring systems, used with reasonable care, can be expected to operate successfully and effectively over substantial intervals and to provide adequate warning that a replacement is in order.

Glossary

Acceptance Rate

The fraction of the total number of applications that are accepted.

Algorithm

"Credit Scoring Algorithm" is the term used by some in place of the term used in this book; "Credit Scoring System". The dictionary definition is: A procedure for solving a mathematical problem in a finite number of steps that frequently involves repetition of an operation; broadly: a step-by-step procedure for solving a problem or accomplishing some end.

Application Score

The number of score points awarded to an applicant based exclusively on the information provided on the application. The points that are derived from information from a credit report are not included. (See Credit Bureau Score and Total Score, below.)

Ascending Cumulative Statistics

A table showing, for each score, what fraction of applicants can be expected to score that score or lower.

Attribute

An item of information about an applicant. These are the possible answers to questions on an application or items of information made available on a credit report. Owning a home is one of the possible attributes of the Characteristic *"Type of Residence"*.

Augmentation

The general term for any process that augments the known Good and Bad accounts in a sample by the Inferred Good and Bad accounts from the applications that were rejected. Also called the Reject Inference.

Bad Rate

The fraction of accepted accounts that perform in an unsatisfactory manner.

Bads

Accounts that the credit grantor wishes he had not accepted. To be useful in the course of constructing a Credit Scoring System, the definition of a Bad account should be stated in terms of observable phenomena regarding time on the books, delinquency, and any other items considered useful.

Behavior Scoring

A scoring system developed using as candidate characteristics the purchase and payment behavior of the individual once he becomes part of the portfolio. While an application scoring system can only be applied once, at the time of application, a behavior scoring system can be applied at regular intervals to form a current estimate of the probability that an account will go Bad.

Characteristic

A question asked on an application or an item of information supplied on a credit report. *Age* is a characteristic, as are *Time at Address*, *Occupation*, and so on. In a behavior scoring system, the characteristics are the various fields in the master record that record payment and purchase performance.

Characteristic Analysis

A comparison of the statistical distribution of counts or percentages of the attributes of characteristics in the current applicant population with those in the sample that was used to develop the system originally.

Classing

Grouping of the attributes used in the Initial Enumeration (see below) to reduce the total number of attributes and to ensure that the sample count in each one is statistically significant.

Coding Instructions

Instructions set down at the time a scoring system is being developed that tell the data entry operators, or the manual coders, how the possible answers to each question (or entry on a credit report), the Characteristics, are to be assigned to the Attributes of the Characteristics.

Once the system is in operation, the people doing the scoring, whether it is done manually or by a computer, must use exactly the same rules. Failure to do so will reduce the power of the scoring system and make evaluation of its effectiveness difficult, if not impossible.

Continuous Characteristic

A Characteristic such as *Age* which has a continuous set of values from, say, 18 to 90. *Income* in dollars is also continuous, as are *Time at Address* or *Time on Job*. (See Discrete Characteristic, below.)

Converted Characteristic

A Characteristic that requires some form of conversion from the raw information provided. For example, weekly salary may be converted into net monthly income, or Age may be converted from Date of Birth and Date of Application. See Characteristics and Generated Characteristic.

Credit Bureau Score

The number of points awarded to an applicant from the information derived from the credit report. In most cases, credit bureau score is calculated after the application score is determined, since in many cases a decision can be reached on Application Score alone, making it unnecessary to spend the time and money on a credit report.

Credit Score

The sum of the points awarded to an applicant for the appropriate attribute of each of the characteristics in a scoring table. If the credit score is at or above the cut-off score (see below) the application is recommended for acceptance, if not, it is recommended for rejection.

Credit Scoring System/Algorithm

A complete scoring product, consisting of the score table and all of the supporting documentation. Also a part of a complete scoring system are the instructional sessions held by the manufacturer (whether the manufacturer is internal or a hired producer) for the benefit of the enterprise planning to use the scoring system.

Cut-off Score

The score below which applications are either automatically rejected or are recommended for rejection.

Descending Cumulative Statistics

A table of scores showing, for each score, the number or percentage of applicants that can be expected to achieve that score or higher.

Discrete Characteristic

A characteristic such as *Occupation* where there is no relationship between the various attributes (answers) that might be provided. Other discrete characteristics are *Bank Relationship*, *Type of Residence*, or *Credit Cards Held*.

Divergence

A measure of the power of a scoring system. The greater the Divergence, the better. Graphically, this is shown by the distance between the means of the score distributions of Good and Bad accounts or applications. In comparing two scoring systems, the one with the greater Divergence is the better of the two.

Dynamic Delinquency Report

A report on delinquent accounts in which accounts that entered the portfolio at different times are compared at equal stages in their account lives. For example, accounts that came on the books at the first quarter of some particular year are compared with those that came on during the second quarter after each of the two groups had been on the books for some specific number of quarters. Such comparisons reveal changes in the behavior of the population comprising the portfolio and suggest questions that management should investigate regarding the causes of change and possible management responses.

ECOA

See Equal Credit Opportunity Act, below.

Equal Credit Opportunity Act (15 USC 1691 *et seq.*)

This is the basic legislation on the Federal level in the United States that addresses credit scoring. It has been amended from time to time. Its principal effect has been to direct the Board of Governors of the Federal Reserve System to develop suitable regulations to enforce the Act. The resulting regulation is known as Regulation B.

Final Score

The score achieved by an applicant after the application score and the credit bureau score have been added together. This final score represents the odds that the applicant will perform in a satisfactory manner.

Fine Classing

See Initial Enumeration, below.

General Credit

Credit extended by a financial institution that permits an individual to use his credit with a variety of sellers or service providers. Visa and Master Cards are examples of General Credit cards, as opposed to captive credit cards such as those issued by a retailer and usable only in that retailer's branches.

Generated Characteristic

A Characteristic generated from two or more others, such as Time at Two Addresses, generated from Time at Address and Time at Previous Address, or Total Family Income, generated by combining all forms of income shown on the application.

Goods

Accounts that a credit grantor is glad he accepted. For the purposes of developing a scoring system, the criteria for a Good account must be objective. Usually, a Good account is defined by stating a minimum time on the books, some minimum use of the credit and some very low level of maximum delinquency at any time in the past.

Indeterminate Accounts

In selecting accepted accounts for inclusion in the body of accounts to be used as the basis for the development of a scoring system, some accounts are found that are neither bad enough to be considered Bad or good enough to be considered Good. For example, an account with too many instances of minor delinquency to be classed as Good but not enough major delinquency to be condiered Bad is classified as indeterminate.

Information Odds

The odds that an applicant will turn out to be a Good account as determined from the information made available about the individual applicant. See Population Odds and Total Odds, below.

Initial Enumeration

The first set of statistical results that are produced in developing a scoring system. The initial enumeration counts all of the data available about the sample cases in as detailed a manner as possible. This is frequently called Fine Classing, since the number of attributes for each characteristic is as large as possible so that the finest structure of the data that is possible can be examined.

Interval Statistics

A table of scoring results that shows, for each score, the number or percent of the applicants that can be expected to achieve that particular score.

Liaison Team

A group of individuals from the organization that is acquiring a credit scoring system that is responsible for communication between the scoring system manufacturer and the user enterprise.

Observation Time

In the development of a Behavior Scoring System, the time at which the status of a group of accounts is observed, those accounts having been selected at some earlier time, called Time Zero.

Odds to be Good

The likelihood that an applicant will develop into an account that performs in a satisfactory manner. This is usually stated in terms such as 10 to 1, meaning that out of 11 applicants, 10 will perform well and one will not.

Overall Odds

The product of the Information Odds and the Population Odds.

Override

An action by a credit grantor by which the decision indicated by the credit scoring system is overriden. There are three types of overrides: Informational, Policy, and Intuitional.

Population

That segment of the customer base of an organization using a credit scoring system to which the scoring system is applied. In a bank there may be several populations, each having its own scoring system. A bank may have one scoring system built on the population that uses credit cards, another for the population that takes out automobile loans, and a third for the population that uses unsecured loans. While these three populations may overlap, they are usually sufficiently different so that different scoring systems make good economic sense.

Population Odds

The underlying odds that a particular population group will perform in a satisfactory manner. This value is usually inferred on the basis of an Augmented population.

Population Stability Index

The calculated value of the Divergence between the original development population and the population that came through the door in a more recent interval.

Population Through the Door

The whole of the population of applicants for a particular credit product from a particular credit grantor. This includes both those that are accepted for credit and those that are rejected.

Reject Inference

See Augmentation.

Restrictions

A requirement placed on the score point calculation program that requires certain conditions to obtain. The most usual case is the restriction that forces the number of score points given to persons 62 years of age and over to be no less that those granted to any other group. Restrictions are sometimes placed on *Occupation* to make the various occupations receive points in a way that is acceptable to the users, or to force continuous characteristics such as *Income* and *Time on Job* to have steadily increasing values even though the statistics might suggest otherwise.

Revalidation

See Validation.

Risk

The likelihood that some event will take place at some time in the future. Usually refers to some undesirable event such as an automobile accident, a fire, or an unsatisfactory credit account. Credit scoring systems provide a numerical measure of risk so that applicants or accounts can be placed in order of increasing risk and the credit grantor can decide on the maximum risk he is willing to accept.

Sample

A body of current or previous accounts that are statistically analyzed to construct a credit scoring system. Both Good and Bad accounts are used in the sample, along with some applications that were rejected.

Score (Total Score)

The sum of the Application Score and the Credit Bureau Score.

Score Card/Score Table

A table listing the characteristics that provide predictive information in the scoring system, the attributes of each characteristic, and the score points associated with each attribute.

Scoring Instructions

The instructions provided to the individuals scoring applications either manually or by machine that instruct them how to associate answers on applications and items on credit reports with attributes used by the scoring system, along with instructions regarding record keeping.

Scoring System/Scoring Algorithm

See Credit Scoring System/Algorithm

Through-the-Door Population

See Population Through the Door.

Total Odds

See Overall Odds.

Validation

A procedure comparing the rank ordering of the quality of accounts of the accepted applicants to the rank ordering predicted by the system at development time. As long as the rank orderings remain substantially the same, the scoring system remains valid.

Index

ADDENDUM

This addendum to the second edition has been inserted so that I can better explain some of the topics that were not adequately covered in the first edition. Most of the deficiencies were detected by my former colleagues at Fair, Isaac and Company who took the trouble to read the book carefully and note the items that, in their view, needed further discussion. I am most grateful to my friends for all the help and encouragement they have given me. The page references indicate the page on which the topic needing discussion is located.

Page 46.

While credit grantors outside the U.S. are not under the specific legal restrictions that are in force in the U.S., almost every country whose economy has a substantial credit component has restrictions of one sort or another to prevent various types of invidious discrimination. In the U.S. a specific body of law has been developed in the credit area. Other countries have anti-discrimination statutes and regulations of varying degrees of formality, not always embodied in one particular statute or regulation. Any credit grantor in any country should take careful legal advice so that he can be sure that he is operating within the limits provided by his own country's laws.

Page 58.

When preparing classed data it is important to examine the Initial Enumeration of the entire sample of accounts, that is, the Rejects as well as the Accepts. Comparison of the Initial Enumerations of the Good/Bad group (all of which were accepted under policies then in force) and the Accept/Reject group may show that there are important differences between the two. It is possible that previous policies acted in a way that resulted in considerable (if unintended) differences between the Accepted and the Rejected groups. Differences of this type must be taken into consideration in the course of constructing the score table.

Page 70.

When some individual characteristic is prevented from entering a scoring system, it is usually the case that one or two others, that otherwise would not have entered, will appear. This is because the sort of characteristics that appear on credit applications or credit files are rarely, if ever, completely independent of each other. While the dependence is not one-for-one, there is usually some significant overlap. For example, an individual who has been on his job for 30 years is very probably older than one who has only been on his for, say, five years. Note that I said "very probably" and not "definitely" since it will not be true in every case. Similarly, a plastic surgeon can usually be expected to have a higher income than an unskilled factory worker.

Almost every pair of characteristics have some degree of overlap. In the case of the Characteristic *Age*, if a requirement is imposed that older individuals receive no fewer points than anyone younger, it is possible that some information will be lost by this restriction, since the actual statistics might lead to a different conclusion. When this happens some other characteristic (or perhaps two) which are in some degree associated with Age and that have not appeared in the scoring system already, will now appear, replacing some, and possibly all, of the information lost when the restriction on Age was imposed.

Page 77.

Both Figures 35 and 36 describe the condition of the credit portfolio at the time the sample data were gathered. These data refer to accounts that came on the books at some time in the past, perhaps as long as three years previously. As a result, the strategy table and the graph in these two figures must be viewed with caution, since the world is not static and it is possible that substantial changes in the applicant population may have taken place in the intervening time. While the options shown in Figure 35 are useful in suggesting possible directions in which policy could move, they must be recognized as pictures of the past rather than as positive predictions of the future.

The strategy curve shown in Figure 36 should be looked at in the same light. The "current strategy" point actually refers to the policy in place at the time the sample was taken and may or may not correspond to the situation at the time the scoring system is delivered.

This being said, the strategy curve shown in Figure 36 is still a most useful device, since it shows the very wide range of opportunity for the credit grantor and at least suggests the possible consequences of various actions. When the scoring system is installed it is up to management to maintain the records that will allow it to establish just how close to current reality the predictions were and how best to take advantage of them.

Page 89.

There is one important case where informational overrides can occur with some frequency. In some cases a scoring system is developed for a bank without taking advantage of the information about applicants for a credit card that may already be in the bank records as a result of their other bank relationships; loans, mortgages, checking or savings accounts, and so on. Such information can be of material use to credit analysts since it can show actual performance with that same institution and can lead to a decision contrary to that recommended by the score.

Page 96.

Since I started this book there have been various advances in the technology of scoring system development. There will, of course, always be such advances and many of the comments made here will lose their immediacy as new ideas are put into action.

A particularly powerful tool that is now available is the hands-on manipulation of the Initial Enumeration data to construct useful and predictive classing. This tool allows a buyer of a scoring system to take a major part in the classing of the data and in deciding how it can best be done in his case. This tool is made even more powerful by the ability to calculate scores quickly so that score tables that result from different approaches to data classing can be compared with relative ease. These tools are becoming more and more powerful and, consequently, more helpful to the end-user in producing a scoring system that meets his particular needs.

Page 101.

While the effect of scores on the entire portfolio cannot be measured immediately, the actual performance of all scored accounts can and should be examined from the time of the installation of the scoring system.

Page 108.

Note that using the same definition for Good and Bad accounts as were used when the scoring system was developed is necessary only when the purpose is to compare the current performance of the system with its performance as predicted at development time. Displays of delinquency by score using various definitions of delinquency are useful in trying to find how these stages of delinquency develop and for deciding how best to deploy the collections effort.

Page 109.

Looking at the performance of accounts shortly after they come on the books can provide early warning of unexpected account behavior. Also, if the expectations of the credit grantor change, perhaps through the acquisition of some new population segment, the earlier the results are examined, the better.

Page 112.

A column effect is not always due to external causes. For example, if a dramatic change is made in collection procedure, this would show up as a column effect. Many of the changes that might take place in an adaptive control environment (see Section III.4) would also cause column effects.

Page 118.

The value of a credit report can be investigated at the time the scoring system is developed. Start with, say, the highest scoring 10% of the sample accounts and compare the total cost of the credit reports that were obtained for them with the loss that might have resulted had the credit grantor accepted those applicants in this group who were turned down because of negative information on the credit report. It is very possible that the total losses from these high scoring rejects (had they been accepted) would have been less than the cost of getting credit reports on the entire group. If that case, buying those reports is not economically justified.

Next, consider the 10% scoring immediately below that highest group and make the same calculation. This process should be continued down the scale of scores until it reaches the point where the losses exceed the cost of the reports and, consequently, making getting reports for that group and for those scoring still lower economically good sense.

Page 124.

This is not strictly the case. Scoring systems are not *absolute* odds quoters, even though they try to be as close as possible. A major reason for this is that the reject inference is imprecise so that the true Population Odds and the Total Odds of which Population Odds are one component, are equally uncertain. This uncertainty is further aggravated by the fact that the Population Odds are subject to change as populations of applicants change.

A more precise statement here would be that accounts that would be expected to behave like other accounts in the rank-ordering of behavior will perform like accounts at a higher, or better performing, place in the overall rank-order.